Working with
DIFFERENCE
& DIVERSITY
in COUNSELLING & PSYCHOTHERAPY

Sara Miller McCune founded SAGE Publishing in 1965 to support the dissemination of usable knowledge and educate a global community. SAGE publishes more than 1000 journals and over 800 new books each year, spanning a wide range of subject areas. Our growing selection of library products includes archives, data, case studies and video. SAGE remains majority owned by our founder and after her lifetime will become owned by a charitable trust that secures the company's continued independence.

Los Angeles | London | New Delhi | Singapore | Washington DC | Melbourne

Working with
DIFFERENCE
& DIVERSITY
in COUNSELLING & PSYCHOTHERAPY

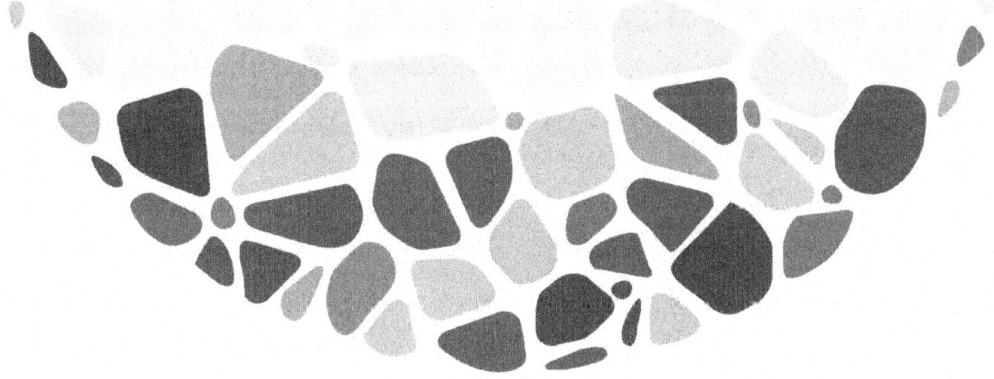

ROSE CAMERON

Los Angeles | London | New Delhi
Singapore | Washington DC | Melbourne

Los Angeles | London | New Delhi
Singapore | Washington DC | Melbourne

SAGE Publications Ltd
1 Oliver's Yard
55 City Road
London EC1Y 1SP

SAGE Publications Inc.
2455 Teller Road
Thousand Oaks, California 91320

SAGE Publications India Pvt Ltd
B 1/I 1 Mohan Cooperative Industrial Area
Mathura Road
New Delhi 110 044

SAGE Publications Asia-Pacific Pte Ltd
3 Church Street
#10-04 Samsung Hub
Singapore 049483

© Rose Cameron 2020

First published 2020

Apart from any fair dealing for the purposes of research or private study, or criticism or review, as permitted under the Copyright, Designs and Patents Act, 1988, this publication may be reproduced, stored or transmitted in any form, or by any means, only with the prior permission in writing of the publishers, or in the case of reprographic reproduction, in accordance with the terms of licences issued by the Copyright Licensing Agency. Enquiries concerning reproduction outside those terms should be sent to the publishers.

Editor: Susannah Trefgarne
Assistant Editor: Ruth Lilly
Production editor: Rachel Burrows
Copyeditor: Christine Bitten
Proofreader: Joanna North
Indexer: Gary Kirby
Marketing manager: Dilhara Attygalle
Cover design: Naomi Robinson
Typeset by: C&M Digitals (P) Ltd, Chennai, India
Printed in the UK

Library of Congress Control Number: 2019954001

British Library Cataloguing in Publication data

A catalogue record for this book is available from the British Library

ISBN 978-1-5264-3664-1
ISBN 978-1-5264-3665-8 (pbk)

At SAGE we take sustainability seriously. Most of our products are printed in the UK using responsibly sourced papers and boards. When we print overseas we ensure sustainable papers are used as measured by the PREPS grading system. We undertake an annual audit to monitor our sustainability.

In memory of Vijay Singh (1979–2018) and Dumah Booker-T James Leach (1953–2017)

Contents

About the Author ix
Acknowledgements xi

Introduction 1

SECTION I THE IMPACT OF 'DIFFERENCE' 3
'Who are you?'

1 The Psychological Impact of Hostility 5
   'That hurt!'

2 The Social Construction of Difference: Race, Ethnicity,
   Nationality and Religion 19
   'You deserved that – you're one of them!'

3 The Social Construction of Difference: Gender, Sex,
   Sexuality, Disability, Age and Class 31
   'I don't like people like you. You're different to me'

4 Reclaiming Identity in the 1970s and 1980s 45
   'This is who we are!'

5 Contemporary Identities 63
   'And we're here too!'

SECTION II BRIDGES AND BARRIERS TO THERAPEUTIC WORK 83
'Can we meet?'

6 Cultural Arrogance 85
   'Shall we meet at my place?'

7 Cultural Humility 93
   'Or shall we meet at your place?'

8 Demonising and Romanticising the 'Other' 103
   'Your place is so far away!'

9 Power and Prejudice 111
   'I can't see you'

10 Power and Privilege   121
    'Don't you know who I am?'

11 Challenges to Communication   133
    'Did you get my message?'

    Conclusion: The Therapeutic Relationship   145
    'We meet at last'

References   149
Index   159

About the Author

Rose Cameron has trained counsellors and psychotherapists in a variety of educational contexts and is currently a Teaching Fellow at the University of Edinburgh. However, she spends most of her working life with clients, and has worked with a wide range of different client groups in her practices in Manchester, Edinburgh, and Fife.

Acknowledgements

The case studies in this book are fictionalised from real situations so my thanks goes to all those who inspired these examples. My thanks also to my family and friends for their patience while I was writing, particularly Ian who tirelessly read and offered feedback on early drafts. Thanks also to the editorial team at SAGE and to Julia Johnson for telling me the (true) story from which I elaborated the allegory that opens the book.

Introduction

This book introduces contemporary theories and debates that are pertinent to working with difference and diversity, and invites you to think about them in relation to your own practice. Professional organisations and educational institutions are increasingly insistent that practitioners pay attention to difference and diversity. The term refers not to individual difference and diversity – every client (and every therapist) is of course unique – but rather to social 'differences' arising from race, ethnicity, religion, gender, gender identity, sexuality, disability, age and class. This emphasis on the client's 'difference' risks suggesting that some clients are different kinds of beings who require something different to 'normal' clients. They do not.

Yet there is a gargantuan body of literature on 'multi-cultural', 'trans-cultural', 'cross-cultural', 'culturally diverse' and 'culturally alert' counselling and psychotherapy. The terms are used synonymously, and while some of this vast literature does, as the terms suggest, discuss culture, much of it is concerned with racism, and as the inclusive terms 'anti-discriminatory' and 'anti-oppressive practice' have come into more common use, with other kinds of discrimination. There is widespread agreement that the potential problem is not the client's 'difference', but the therapist's attitude towards that difference. Most of us have intellectual and emotional work to do if we are to offer the same quality of service to all clients. This book aims to challenge and support you in thinking about differences that you would rather not acknowledge and to reflect upon your understanding of, and attitude towards, those that you do.

The language of this literature is currently being augmented by the terms 'social justice' and 'human rights'. (The term 'social justice' is used in relation to working with clients who are in some way socially disadvantaged, and 'human rights' is usually used in relation to working with asylum seekers.) Psychotherapy and counselling have long been criticised for failing to take account of the social context in which clients become distressed or disturbed. The criticism is that personal problems often have their origins in social problems such as poverty, inequality of opportunity, demeaning social imagery and other forms of social hostility, but are framed, in therapy, as having a psychological origin within the individual, thus reducing the impetus for much needed social change. Social justice and human rights approaches encourage therapists to advocate on behalf of clients, both on an individual and a wider political level.

Working with difference and diversity involves understanding our clients, ourselves and the therapeutic relationship within a context of power-laden social relationships.

It demands that we look at the bigger picture; that we develop a good enough understanding of how clients are impacted by social injustice; how we ourselves are impacted by social injustice; and also how we, in our work as therapists, may resist or collude with constructing and perpetuating some of these injustices. As illustrated in this book, the mental health professions have a history of colluding with the creation and perpetuation of injustice and suffering. It is important to understand our personal history in order to avoid harming a client, and it is important to understand the history of our profession in order to avoid repeating history by inflicting mass misery through practices such as conversion therapy.

Our professional ancestors, the early psychologists who attributed intellectual and moral qualities to different races, participated in one of the most brutal mechanisms of exploitation and abuse. This book acknowledges our historic collective professional responsibility in helping to create ideas and practices that caused intense and widespread suffering. It invites you to think about how the profession that you are joining, or are already a member of, interacts with the wider community and how we currently support or challenge its inequalities.

Working with difference and diversity is about broadening one's horizons and becoming increasingly able to understand things from a different perspective. This book engages with a range of literature in order to help you do so. Whether we are aware of it or not, the ways in which we, as therapists and as members of the larger social world, think about race, ethnicity, gender, sexuality, disability, class, culture and power are very much determined by ideas from social sciences such as sociology and anthropology. Some of these ideas are now considered out-dated in the academic disciplines in which they originated and so this book introduces contemporary ideas. The book also recommends pieces of journalism, memoirs and works of fiction that speak to us of the 'other'.

One of the frequent criticisms of much of the cross-cultural and anti-discriminatory literature is that in assuming that the therapist is white and middle class it does not address therapists with marginalised social identities. This book assumes that you have a multiplicity of social identities, some of which may be mainstream, and some marginalised.

A note on the typeface

The body text in this book is typeset in a sans serif font in the hope that this will make it more user-friendly for dyslexic readers.

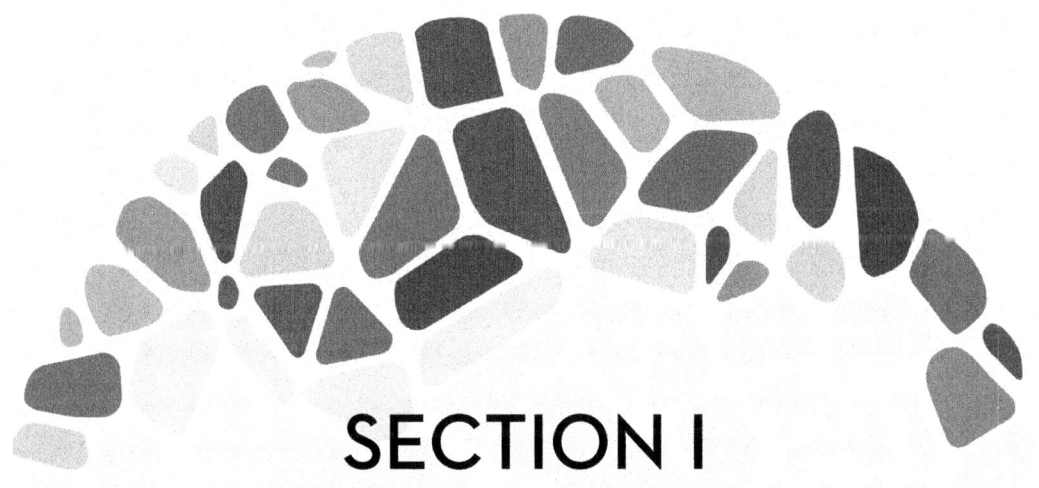

SECTION I

THE IMPACT OF 'DIFFERENCE'

'WHO ARE YOU?'

1
The Psychological Impact of Hostility

'That hurt!'

Learning aims

- To appreciate the psychological stress that results from living in a hostile environment, and to consider its impact on your clients, and yourself.
- To think about the issues involved in working both with those who suffer hostility and those who perpetrate it.
- To understand and be able to work therapeutically with the relational and psychological processes involved in being 'us' and 'them'.
- To consider how the concepts of microaggressions, ethnocultural allodynia, race-based traumatic stress injury, intergenerational transmission of trauma and minority stress might inform your work.

> **An allegory**
>
> I was once told a story about a man – I'll call him Zeno – who became convinced that his neighbour was carrying out a systematic campaign of hostility against him, spreading vicious and demeaning rumours about him and using all sorts of subtle ploys to damage his family, his career and his reputation. Zeno claimed that his neighbour posted excrement through his letterbox, and even that he had posted a burning paraffin-soaked rag in an attempt to kill him.
>
> He complained to the police, and then complained that the police were also persecuting him. His friends and colleagues didn't know whether to believe him or not. Eventually, he was persuaded to see a doctor. The doctor, who was patient and kind, did not believe him. Zeno became adamant, insistent, then agitated and angry. The doctor called security. Zeno was admitted to hospital involuntarily, diagnosed with paranoid schizophrenia and given antipsychotic medication.
>
> The medication made him feel calmer and he eventually continued with his treatment on a voluntary basis. One day he was talking about something his neighbour had done when the psychiatrist suddenly asked him exactly what his address was. She had recognised the street he'd been describing and remembered that she had another paranoid schizophrenic patient who lived there. It transpired that this other patient was Zeno's neighbour – and had indeed been carrying out a campaign of hostility against him.

The above story seems like a fitting allegory for the psychological impact of being subjected to hostility on the basis of one's nationality, ethnicity, race, class, gender, sexuality, ethnicity, disability or religion. Until the upsurge in overt hostility and violence towards marginalised people following the 2016 Brexit referendum in Britain and the election of Donald Trump in the USA, many people thought hostility and discrimination were things of the past. The idea that we are 'post-race' was clearly delusional as evidenced by the need for a movement that points out that black lives matter as much as white lives – in Britain as well as in the USA (McVeigh, 2016; Cole, 2018). In 2012, Theresa May, who was then Home Secretary, announced a 'hostile environment' policy towards those who failed to convince the Home Office of their need for asylum. The Windrush scandal revealed, in 2018, that May's message – 'you're not one of "us", and you're not welcome' – was also being directed at people who are British citizens – black British citizens – and that the policy was used to illegally threaten and deport them (Davey, 2019).

Nor are we post-class. The way that we think about class may be changing (as discussed in the next chapter), but economic inequality is more prevalent since the banking crisis of 2008 and subsequent policy of austerity. The language used in public discourse once again includes 'the poor'. The United Nations Special Rapporteur on extreme poverty and human rights (Alston, 2019) found 14 million people living in poverty in the UK (that's a fifth of the population) with

1.5 million classed as destitute, unable to afford essential basics like food or dental care.

The Special Rapporteur, who concluded that poverty in the UK could be ended if there was the political will to do so, was particularly critical of the introduction of the single monthly social security payment, Universal Credit, which, he said, left people destitute and in despair. Although austerity has hit those already poor the hardest, the introduction and administration of Universal Credit has, he says, pushed other groups into poverty. He highlighted the impact upon women, racial and ethnic minorities, children, single parents and people with disabilities. Ryan (2019) confirms the impact upon disabled people, and other commentators have highlighted the impact upon those leaving care (The Children's Society, 2017), dying (Youle, 2019) or in poor mental health (Matthews-King, 2019). The UN Rapporteur found that the reformed benefits system discriminates against women so badly that if a roomful of misogynists had set out to create a system that works for men but not women they would not have had to add much (Ward, 2018).

The government has been instrumental in creating a hostile atmosphere for those perceived as 'not us', as 'other' on account of their income, nationality, ethnicity, race, class, gender, sexuality, disability, religion or whether they have a permanent home. However, the government is not wholly responsible for the hostile atmosphere in which the 'other' lives. The message that you're not one of 'us' and you're not welcome here is also conveyed through less overt social channels. We all create and sustain the idea of 'difference' in the ways in which 'we' relate to the 'other'. 'We' constantly give 'them' subliminal – or sometimes overt – messages about who has more social status, who is 'better', who is – and is not – welcome, who is one of 'us' and who is one of 'them'.

Therapy, which is itself a relationship of unequal power, takes place in this wider context of unequal social relationships. The ways in which society moulds our relationship to each other outside the therapy room inevitably sneak into the therapy room. The social identities of both therapist and client form a background to the therapeutic relationship, which is never comprised of simply a therapist and a client, but a white therapist and a black client, or a female therapist and a male client, or a gay therapist and a gay client, etc.

This chapter assumes that most readers have both marginalised and mainstream social identities. As it looks at abusive social power relationships – and the challenge is to avoid enacting these in therapy – it may be most useful to engage with the chapter from your mainstream positions, whatever these may be – for example, if you are gay and middle class, by reading in relation to your class position.

Microaggressions

The term 'microaggressions' refers to words and actions that wound although they are not necessarily intended to do so (or at least not consciously intended). The term was initially used in relation to racism, but is now used to also describe the under-hand hostility experienced by people from other marginalised groups. Microaggressions include:

1. **Microassaults** include conscious discrimination, using denigrating language and avoiding contact with particular groups. Avoiding working with clients from a marginalised group because you don't feel comfortable with 'them' would be an example of a microassault (this, of course, is different from avoiding working with clients from a marginalised group because you know that you have an antipathy towards 'them' and you're not over it yet, but you are working on it).
2. **Microinsults** include rudeness, subtle snubs and veiled insults. Clients may be routinely excluded and insulted in ways that are invisible to the therapist, both outside and within the therapy room. Microinsults have a cumulative impact. The working-class women with whom the sociologist Beverley Skeggs (1997) researched class identities, for instance, recounted feeling so unwelcome in 'high end' shops that they eventually stopped going into the city centre.

> **Reflective exercise**
>
> One of the participants in Skeggs's research is in therapy with you. How might you conceptualise her avoidance of the city centre? Does this conceptualisation take account of the reality of class hostility or have you pathologised your client's avoidance? How might you work with her avoidance in a way that takes account of the reality of class hostility while also creating the potential for a different response?

- 'Mansplaining' is another kind of microinsult. The term specifies the way in which men often assume ignorance on a woman's part and carefully explain either the patently obvious or something that the woman already understands perfectly well. However, being patronising is not a purely male prerogative. Ignorance and/or stupidity are also assumed on the basis of class, race, age, disability and ethnicity.
- Microinsults emerge from an absence of respect and not only poison the therapeutic relationship but are themselves anti-therapeutic. Hopefully you will not be intentionally rude, dismissive or more subtly aggressive towards a client, but any disrespect that your client perceives must be listened to properly and understood from the client's position both within the therapeutic relationship and within society. You must also be willing to examine yourself.

> **Case study**
>
> Miriam arrived for supervision with a lot of trepidation because a client had taken offence when she had asked him if he could read. When we explored this, Miriam was initially insistent that she had needed to find out if the client could read the contract and assessment questionnaire. We talked about it

> being good practice to go through a contract verbally with all clients, and about the advantages of making an assessment questionnaire a relational endeavour. There was something more. Miriam looked uncomfortable, then acknowledged that she had assumed that her client was probably illiterate.
>
> When she reflected on why she'd felt the need to ask rather than just taking the more graceful (and useful) route of going through the paperwork together, she got in touch with an uncomfortable feeling of spite. Miriam had, depending on how you imagined her, grown up hearing pitying references to the lack of education amongst her client's ethnic group, or she was of the same ethnic group as her client, but from a more privileged, and educated, layer of society. Either way, her question had really been a little sting. She was reluctant to acknowledge this to her client (despite the client undoubtedly having felt the sting) but did apologise to him for making an assumption about him.
>
> She took her feeling of spite to her own therapy. She realised quite quickly that it was a defence against her own class-based feelings of inferiority. Both diminished over time.

   Those who are not used to being treated with respect really notice its presence. A client whom I saw in an NHS setting said, when we were reviewing our relationship prior to saying goodbye, that one of the most important things I'd done was to approach him and quietly ask if he was waiting to see me when we first met, rather than bawling his name across a crowded waiting room.

3. **Microinvalidations** include negating, nullifying or otherwise not accepting someone's experience of hostility. This might take the form of suggesting that they are perhaps over-reacting or being over-sensitive. Exclusion hurts. Judgment hurts. Put-downs hurt. Lillian Comas-Díaz and Frederick Jacobsen (2001) borrow the term *allodynia* from medicine, where it refers to the way in which we become physically very sensitive if previously hurt – the slightest knock is really painful if you're already bruised. They use the term 'ethnocultural allodynia' to describe the heightened sensitivity that comes with repeated abuse on the basis of race and ethnicity.

   They also discuss clients being 'over-sensitive', seeing hostility where there is none. This idea is more problematic as it focuses on the intention of the perpetrator rather than the experience of the recipient. Whether someone who banged into my already bruised knee did so accidentally or semi-deliberately is not my immediate concern. My immediate concern is the excruciating pain that I feel. Yet when it comes to abusive social relationships, the concern seems to be overwhelmingly for the person who feels accused, especially if they are accused of racism – and their concern also seems to be for themselves. The already tender knee that hurts so badly is overlooked.

The idea that a client may sometimes see hostility where there is none is also problematic because it is true, but not all of the time. Perhaps the most useful thing we can do as practitioners (and as people) is to remember that microaggressions are underplayed, subtle, discreet, ambiguous. The very nature of a microaggression is that it may look and sound innocent. But they sting anyway, regardless of intention.

> **Reflective exercise**
>
> Reflect, alone or with others, on any instances in which you thought that a client was being over-sensitive with regard to a perceived slight on account of their race, ethnicity, gender, gender identity, sexuality or religion, and/or an instance in which you wondered if you were being over-sensitive to a similar remark made by a client.

Microinvalidations deny or dismiss a marginalised client's experience of hostility. Zeno was not paranoid; his neighbour really was out to get him. Skeggs's research participants really were unwelcome in the high-end shop. Responding to a client's experience of being subjected to hostility by assuming that they misperceived what was going on would be a microinvalidation, or in more recent terminology, 'gaslighting', a term that refers to George Dewey Cukor's film *Gaslight* (1944) in which a man constantly denies his wife's experience as a means of making her doubt her grip on reality (she gets her revenge).

Assuming that one's own mainstream beliefs and values are more valid or true than a marginalised client's beliefs and values, is also a microinvalidation.

> **Reflective exercise**
>
> What are your personal and professional views on:
>
> - Fate/God's will
> - Spirits that can be seen and conversed with
> - Frightening spirits
> - Prayer
> - Magic

> **Reflective exercise**
>
> Mrs Wilson is an older woman, originally from Jamaica. She has been talking about a friend who died a few weeks ago and casually mentions that she saw her in the street the other day. You establish that she is talking about *duppy* (a kind ghost but not inherently frightening). What do your immediate and your more considered responses say about your ability to take other realities seriously?

Microinvalidations are often nonverbal, for example, looking bored while a client is complaining of being treated unfairly, punctuating your listening with an exasperated sigh. The context is, of course, all-important. The conscious intent less so. Microinsults and microinvalidations are often an unconscious expression of an attitude that we are not aware of holding, and may conflict with our concept of ourselves in that we do not see ourselves or our attitudes as hostile.

Microaggressions are powerful precisely because they are covert, ambiguous and easily denied. Microaggressions are, in some ways, more difficult to process than overt hostility, especially when they come from someone one trusted. Because microaggressions are not overt and are easily denied, they are usually described as 'subtle'. 'Sneaky' or even 'snide' might sometimes be more appropriate terms. Microaggressions are poisoned darts. They're nasty, they're sneaky and they leave a dirty wound. The cumulative effects of the snide can be as corrosive as the overt and violent. They feed the hostile atmosphere in which some of our clients live, and they can sneak into the therapy room.

Reflective exercise

Depending on whether you are working alone or with others, think, write or talk about your experience of directing any of the above microaggressions against a client (or someone else). Were you aware at the time of potentially causing offence? What was the larger context? What are your feelings about it now?

Being hated hurts

Psychotherapeutic theory has been somewhat slow to recognise that being subjected to on-going hostility on account of one's 'difference' has a psychological impact. The concept of 'minority stress', which is still better known in the USA than the UK, comes from a union of social science and psychology research and posits that those marginalised on account of their 'difference' suffer chronically high levels of stress. Minority stress theory distinguishes between external or 'distal' stressors, which include experiences of discrimination and other forms of hostility, and internal or 'proximal' stressors.

External stressors include stereotypes, and in fact, the social psychologist Claude Steele (2010) has shown that 'stereotype threat' – being reminded that you may be judged in accordance with a negative stereotype – can dramatically affect how well you do things. This is true for anyone, including mainstream groups, but affects people from marginalised groups more frequently because negative stereotypes of them are bandied around more freely in public life.

Internal stressors include feeling anxious that you might be subjected to hostility, being hyper-vigilant, hiding one's marginalised identity (for example, being 'in the closet') and having negative feelings about one's own marginalised group and marginalised identity (for example, internalised homophobia, internalised racism, etc.). The chronic stress that these culminate in leads to health inequalities with more people from marginalised groups suffering from physical and psychological conditions than their mainstream counterparts.

Robert Carter (1995) discusses how the impact of on-going hostility accumulates and a trauma reaction can be triggered by a relatively minor 'last straw' event. His Race-Based Traumatic Stress Injury model differs from the Post Traumatic Stress Disorder (PTSD) model in that the core stressor is emotional pain rather than threat to life (people do, of course suffer racial assaults that threaten their lives, and these have always – in theory at least – been recognised as causing Post Traumatic Stress Disorder).

Carter is interested in having the psychological damage done to those subjected to racism recognised, rather than medicalised. He is very clear that the *intrusion* (recurring thoughts), *avoidance* (not being able to think about it), *arousal* (irritability), anxiety, anger, rage, depression, low self-esteem, shame and guilt that result from being subjected to racism do not constitute a disorder. Carter is ahead of his time (still). Post Traumatic Stress is, in DSM 5, still a disorder but there are moves afoot to have it re-categorised as a syndrome, and therefore substantially de-medicalised.

The term 'syndrome' – 'a condition characterised by a set of associated symptoms' (Oxford English Dictionary) – still medicalises distress that has a social cause. In doing so, it reconceptualises a social problem as an individual problem, thus dismissing the need for social change. A social justice approach to working with difference and diversity calls upon us to challenge this obfuscation.

Although the diagnostic criteria for PTSD have, in DSM 5, been widened to acknowledge the possibility of a delayed reaction, the criterion of a particular and 'big' experience remains, and so the cumulative effects of low-key, long-term hostility are not recognised in this diagnosis. However, DSM 5 does recognise that:

- racism can have a negative impact on mental health
- there is evidence that racism can exacerbate and prolong many psychiatric disorders
- practitioner bias may influence diagnoses.

DSM 5 also recognises that the disproportionate diagnosis of PTSD in girls and women may be due, in part, to gender-based violence, but does not consider the cumulative stress of living with non-violent, on-going exclusion and hostility on account of one's gender – or class, religion, disability, sexuality, etc. This is important to practitioners in the UK as well as the USA because DSM is widely used here – and because the eleventh edition of the International Classification of Diseases (ICD-11: the European DSM) makes no mention of racism or any other system of hostility.

Intergenerational transmission of trauma

Not only is psychological stress subtly ingrained in the present; it also seeps through from the past. The intergenerational transmission of trauma – passing the effects of trauma down from one generation to the next – was first recognised in the children of Holocaust survivors.

Lillian Comas-Díaz and Beverley Greene (1994) use the term 'Complex Post-Colonisation Stress Disorder' in describing the devastating psychological effects of living under colonisation, both past and present. These include identity confusion, alienation, self-denial, somatic symptoms, depression, shame, rage, relational difficulties, becoming demoralised and losing hope. Comas-Díaz's (2000) 'psychotherapeutic decolonisation' involves helping clients examine beliefs and attitudes that reinforce the colonised mentality (e.g. that the colonising people are superior – or, conversely, that the colonisers were 'bad' while the colonised 'good'), to help clients develop a positive and integrated identity and to increase autonomy and dignity. The therapeutic relationship is central as the therapist bears witness to the client's story.

Minority stress

The concept of minority stress was originally developed to help explain health inequalities in sexual and racial minorities, and most of the research still pertains to these groups although the concept can also be usefully applied to other marginalised people. Being subjected to hostility is bad for you, whatever your 'difference'. Living with the psychological stress of unprocessed outrage, anger, fear, shame and hopelessness is bad for you. It is therefore essential that the therapeutic relationship is a safe, secure and containing space in which clients can process these feelings. This means that the therapist must be unafraid both of the strength of their client's feelings and of properly recognising the harsh social realities that gives rise to them.

> **Reflective exercise**
>
> Imagine (or remember) a client being really, really angry with the social group that subjects them to hostility (and of which you are a member). What feelings arise in you? Imagine (or remember) a client feeling helplessness, despair and exhaustion in relation to on-going low-grade hostility that they are subjected to. What feelings arise in you? Imagine (or remember) a client feeling intense shame about not defending themselves against a (physical or psychological) attack. What feelings arise in you? Where might you work with the feelings aroused by these scenarios? Personal therapy? Supervision? A development group? Make plans to do so.

Was Zeno driven mad by his neighbour's hostility? Was he really suffering from paranoid schizophrenia by the time he was hospitalised? If he was black, he was certainly likely to be given this diagnosis. In recounting the story, I used a man rather than a gender-neutral 'somebody' in recognition of the fact that paranoid schizophrenia is a diagnosis that is given disproportionately to black men. Black people of all genders are up to 12 times more likely to be diagnosed with schizophrenia, and black men are more likely than black women to be given a diagnosis of paranoid schizophrenia (Harrison et al., 1988; see also Howitt and Owusu-Bempah, 1994).

There are a number of factors that are thought to contribute to racially disproportionate diagnoses, including practitioners misunderstanding cultural and religious practices and beliefs, practitioners readily perceiving black men as aggressive and threatening, and the racialised nature of the diagnostic criteria. Jonathan Metzi (2010) describes how the diagnostic criteria for schizophrenia changed during the American Civil Rights era. The criteria had previously painted a very subdued picture and the diagnosis was mostly given to white, middle-class women (inconvenient wives, perhaps). During the Civil Rights era, schizophrenia became associated with protest (there was actually a psychiatric 'illness' called 'protest schizophrenia'). The diagnostic picture became angry, male, potentially violent – and black.

The potential ending to Zeno's story – that the psychiatrist merely shrugs her shoulders at the coincidence of two patients with the same diagnosis living next door to each other, or that she discharges Zeno and admits his neighbour, or that she admits the neighbour and also offers Zeno some therapy to help him recover from being subjected to a campaign of hostility – is a political issue that concerns all of us who work with mental health issues.

Education, campaigning and political action, both within the profession and wider society, are necessary if we do not want the ending in which the psychiatrist merely shrugs her shoulders. It is important to be sensitised to the impact of social inequality in the privacy of the therapy room as well as in the wider world. However, it is also important that an understanding of social inequality and its impact *informs* therapeutic practice rather than replaces it. Clients come to therapy for therapy, not to be impressed by their therapist's political analysis, nor to be recruited for the revolution.

Hating hurts too

Arbitrary hatred, campaigns of systematic hostility, the spreading of vicious and demeaning rumours and posting burning rags through letter boxes is as indicative of racism and other systems of hatred as it is of paranoid schizophrenia. Might this suggest that racism is an illness?

Moves towards having racism classified as a mental disorder began during the American Civil Rights movement of the 1960s, and initially came from black psychiatrists who had been working with black patients impacted by a spate of racist killings. Their request to have extreme bigotry classified as a mental disorder was turned down by the American Psychiatric Association (APA) on the grounds that extreme racism in the USA is not unusual and therefore a social rather than a psychiatric problem (Poussaint, 2002). The APA also expressed concern that classifying racism as a psychiatric disorder might encourage perpetrators to perceive what is actually a chosen political stance as being beyond their choice and control.

As the 1970s brought a backlash against the struggle for equality in the USA, the idea that racism is an illness with a genetic basis, or a manifestation of a 'natural' fear of people outside one's own group was advanced by sociobiologists. There has, since then, been a swell of research, treatment models and theoretical frameworks pointing in the direction of understanding racism as a pathology that can be effectively treated through behaviour modification and, perhaps, medication (see, for example, Terbeck et al., 2012). The danger in treating extreme prejudice as a psychiatric illness, as Gates (1990) points out, is that medication acts as a social painkiller, masking the social, political and economic conditions that perpetuate discrimination and hostility.

> **Reflective exercise**
>
> Zeno's neighbour has not been given a diagnosis after all, and is seeing you rather than a psychiatrist. He initially alluded to 'actions' that he has been involved in. It becomes clear that these 'actions' are hate crimes. You strongly suspect that he has already caused others serious harm and that he currently constitutes a serious threat to others.
>
> Depending on whether you are working alone or with others, think, write or talk about the ethical issues that might arise as you work with this client and how you might address them. You may want to consider the following:
>
> Do you have a duty to protect the wider community? If so, how might you do so?
>
> Does it make a difference whether the harm you imagine is physical or psychological?
>
> Do you consider this client to be mentally ill? Do you think he ought to be considered ill by psychiatric services? What might the consequences be of considering him ill, both for your client and for the rest of society?
>
> If you do not consider him to be ill, might you consider breaking confidentiality to the police? At what point? What would your client need to tell you? What would the police need to know in order for your disclosure to be justified? Would you tell your client that you were going to break confidentiality?
>
> If you were to decide not to break confidentiality and the therapeutic relationship remained intact, how might you work with your client's attitudes?

You may have reached a difficult impasse with the exercise above. Not all problems are easily solved, but they nevertheless warrant consideration. This exercise is (loosely) based upon my own work with a client, who, at the time that we worked together, was regretful (and vague) about hate crimes that he may have committed in the past. I did not break his confidentiality. I recently learned that he had later been imprisoned for a horrifically violent attack. The questions that I posed in the exercise are the sort of questions I have been thinking about ever since. They have real-life implications for our clients, and for ourselves as therapists and as members of society.

I was still in training while seeing this client. Shortly before we started working together, I had participated in a training exercise in which I was asked what kinds of clients I thought I would be unable to work with. My answer had been 'fascists' (it was the 1980s). I was initially unaware of my client's varied and extreme hatreds, but once he brought them to therapy as something that he had moved away from, but wanted to explore, I found that I was glad we were working together. I believed that our work would, in a very tiny way, make the world a safer place. Clearly I was wrong. I was also shaken. I hope that, once I've processed this some more, I can retrieve enough hope to try again if the opportunity ever presents itself.

Reflective exercise

Another of Zeno's neighbours comes to see you (he doesn't know the first neighbour – it's a long street – so there is no boundary issue). His presenting problem concerns bereavement, but it becomes very evident he is racist, sexist, homophobic, transphobic, Islamophobic and condescending towards disabled people and elderly people. How might you feel about working with him? Do you see his prejudices as a therapeutic issue? If you do, how might you conceptualise them from within your theoretical framework and how might you work with them? If you do not see them as a therapeutic concern, why not?

Conclusion

The debate as to whether extreme racism is a psychiatric disorder looks set to continue. However, there is, from a psychotherapeutic (as opposed to a biomedical) point of view, no need to set the social and the psychological in competition with each other. Racism and other systems of social abuse can be understood as a social, political, economic *and* psychological construction. Rather than understanding racism and other systems of hate as a chemical imbalance in the brain (or rooted in a 'natural' fear of strangers), it is perhaps more useful to understand 'us and them thinking' as the projection of what is feared and hated in the self onto the 'other'. The next chapter looks at how various social identities have been created through constructing some groups as 'different', and how 'us and them' thinking has stigmatised those construed as 'different', while, paradoxically, denying the diversity of human beings.

Further reading

Challenges to the medical model of mental 'illness'

Cooke, A. (2017) Understanding Psychosis and Schizophrenia: Why People Sometimes Hear Voices, Believe Things that Others Find Strange, or Appear out of Touch with Reality, and What Can Help. Leicester: British Psychological Society. Available at: www1.bps.org.uk/system/files/Public%20files/rep03_understanding_psychosis.pdf (accessed 15 February 2019).

Read, J. and Dillon, J. (eds) (2013) Models of Madness: Psychological, Social and Biological Approaches to Psychosis, 2nd edn. London: Routledge.

And a psychodynamic article about working therapeutically with schizophrenia:

Karon, B.P. (2003) 'The tragedy of schizophrenia without psychotherapy', *Journal of the American Academy of Psychoanalysis*, 31(1): 89–118.

On the wounds of racism

Bains, S. (2011) 'Racism as trauma', in C. Lago and B. Smith (eds), *Anti-Discriminatory Practice in Counselling & Psychotherapy*. London: Sage. pp. 23–32.

Kinouani, G. (2019) 'Working with racial trauma in psychotherapy', *Therapy Today*, 30(8): 36–9.

Menakem, R. (2017) *My Grandmother's Hands: Racialized Trauma and the Pathways to Mending Our Hearts and Bodies*. Las Vegas: Central Recovery Press.

On the wounds of class

Gorman, T.J. (2017) *Growing up Working Class: Hidden Injuries and the Development of Angry White Men and Women*. Basingstoke: Palgrave Macmillan.

Not a recent paper, but still relevant:

Russell, G. (1996) 'Internalized classism', *Women & Therapy*, 18(3–4): 59–71.

On transgenerational trauma

Charny, I.W. (1995) *Holding on to Humanity – The Message of Holocaust Survivors: The Shamai Davidson Papers*. New York: New York University Press.

Tsitsi Dangarembga's semiautobiographical trilogy, set in Zimbabwe (then Rhodesia) begins in the 1970s, and explores the complex impact of colonialism on identity and relationships:

Dangarembga, T. (2004 [1988]) *Nervous Conditions*. Banbury: Ayebia Clarke.

Dangarembga, T. (2006) *The Book of Not*. Banbury: Ayebia Clarke.
Dangarembga, T. (2018) *This Mournable Body*. Minneapolis: Graywolf Publishers.

Dinaw Mengestu's novel can also be read as a study of intergenerational trauma:

Mengestu, D. (2010) *How to Read the Air*. London: Jonathan Cape.

2
The Social Construction of Difference: Race, Ethnicity, Nationality and Religion

'You deserved that – you're one of them!'

Learning aims

- To understand how the idea of race and racial differences came into being. This provides a conceptual base with which to understand some of the ideas discussed in later chapters. It also provides a cognitive basis from which to begin changing your own prejudices and biases.
- To cultivate critical professional awareness by understanding how our professional ancestors contributed to the creation of race.
- To appreciate that the politics of inclusion and exclusion is inherent in the construction of race.
- To reflect on the construction of your own racial identity.

The previous chapter discussed the psychological impact of being subjected to hostility on the basis of a perceived 'difference'. These 'differences' are often believed to be 'natural' – some groups are thought to be 'naturally' different from others – different in nature, essentially different. These 'differences' are neither natural, nor essential, but rather ideas that have become ingrained in our way of seeing the world.

There is, for example, nothing 'natural' about race. The idea that the human race can be sub-divided into different races of people who are biologically alike and different to people of other races is nonsense. However, until recently, most people were brought up with this idea and so have a vague understanding that racial differences are biological. They are not.

This can be difficult to understand given that the colour of your skin, the texture of your hair and the shape of your eyes are clearly biological attributes, and so this chapter explains the social construction of race at some length. It ends by clarifying the distinctions between race, ethnicity, nationality and religion.

The invention of race

Modern race theory began as European colonialists came into contact with people in different parts of the world. Naturalists – philosophers of the natural world and early scientists – categorised people on the basis of where they came from and what they looked like. The differences that these early – and subsequent – race theorists observed were not a mere description of what was there, but a matter of perception. We are so used to thinking in terms of race, that racial differences can seem self-evident. They are not; they depend upon perspective, as evidenced by the fact that different observers saw from 2, to 3, 4, 5, 6, 7, 8, 11, 15, 16, 22, 60 and 63 different races, or to use the terms more prevalent at the time, 'types', or 'species'.

Five of the racial categories that are commonly used today when studying human migration and identifying human remains – Caucasian, Mongoloid, Malay, Negroid and American Indian – were created (and I do mean 'created' rather than 'identified') by Johann Friedrich Blumenbach between 1793 and 1795; Australoid was added in the 1940s, and the Capoid race (i.e. the Khoi and San people of Southern Africa) was added in 1962.

Despite the air of scientific authority that these categorisations have conferred on the concept of race, racial categorisation remains a matter of perception. In Britain, 'Asian' usually means that you, or your forebears, come from India, Pakistan, Bangladesh, Sri Lanka or another country in South Asia, whereas in the USA 'Asian' usually means that you, or your forebears, come from China, Japan, Korea, Taiwan, the Philippines or another country in East Asia.

How race is assigned has varied over time and place. In some countries, it is or was based upon heritage, and in other countries upon appearance. The same person may still be considered black in one place and white in another. It is one thing to understand this cognitively, and another thing to experience a challenge to your perception. You may find the following exercise disconcerting.

> **Reflective exercise**
>
> Listen to: http://stateofthereunion.com/pike-county-oh-as-black-as-we-wish-to-be/, and/or do an online search for images of William Cross, the African American scholar whose work on developing a positive black identity is introduced in Chapter 3.

Professor Cross is indeed the white-looking man with a nose so sharp it could cut paper. If you came across the YouTube video of him giving a Distinguished Psychologist Address (Fairchild, 2012) and got past the first few minutes of acknowledgements, you will have heard him talking about looking different to the rest of his family, along with whom he grew up, as black, under 'Jim Crow', the laws that segregated black and white people after the abolition of slavery in the USA.

The 'one drop rule' decreed that anyone who had any African ancestry was black (or, rather 'negro', since Cross and other activists were yet to replace the term with 'black'). In Britain, race is determined by what somebody looks like – their racial phenotype. Having 'negro blood' did not make Cross 'look black' and looking white did not make him white. Race is a social experience, not a biological fact.

Shah (2019) confirms that the family in the state of the reunion audio file suggested above, all of whom have pale skin and red hair, have birth certificates that say that they are black because of the 'one drop rule'. Most of the family consider themselves black and are considered to be so by others, yet one of the daughters considers herself to be white, and, when at school in another town, is considered by others to be white. 'Race' is a community perception.

Race theory was not merely a matter of arranging people into categories: these categories had – and still have – social meaning. Early naturalists arranged the 'races' or 'types' into hierarchies of humanness, civilisation and proximity to the Divine. Lives were valued accordingly: human over the bestial; civilised over the barbaric; Christian over heathen.

The model for this racial hierarchy – the medieval notion of a 'Great Chain of Being' in which all of Creation is related in a strict hierarchy with God at the top, followed by angels, people, animals, plants and rocks at the bottom – was influential in race theory. The idea that non-European peoples were a missing link in the Chain between human beings and animals was used to justify the brutalities of colonisation, slavery and genocide. A 'savage' was not fully human. Indigenous peoples were hunted as animals are, and it was perfectly acceptable to kill a slave just for the hell of it until the Catholic Church, and some time later, the Protestant Church, eventually conceded that slaves (who were, by then, exclusively African) also have souls, and are therefore human.

Many naturalists thought that the different races they had identified must have different origins, and in fact, the word 'race' comes from the Latin for 'origin'. The naturalist and zoologist Georges Cuvier, for instance, thought that Adam and Eve were Caucasian and that the other races came into being after survivors from a major catastrophe fled in different directions and subsequently developed in isolation from each other (Jackson and Weidman, 2005). Others, including Charles Darwin, thought that all human beings had a common origin. Even after Darwin's theory of evolution had become widely accepted, the debate continued, the question becoming whether we all became human at once or whether different races emerged from different ancestors. The multiple origin theory has not entirely gone away. Carlton Coon (Coon, 1962), the President of the American Association of Physical Anthropologists argued, as recently as 1962, that different races evolved into *Homo sapiens* separately, and the idea is authoritatively touted on the Internet.

Race theorists became interested in *how* races differed as well as *why* they differed. Skulls were measured by craniometrists; body parts measured by anthropometrists; and bodily fluids analysed by serologists. Race became about biology. The idea that difference was innate and could be located in our blood – or skulls – had been growing in strength since the end of the Middle Ages. The idea that children had the same 'blood' as their parents laid the foundation for ideas about the 'purity' of 'bloodlines'. These ideas racialised hatreds that had previously been about religion. The Spanish Inquisition, for instance, didn't care if a Jew had converted to Christianity – they still had to prove the 'purity' of their 'blood' (Hannaford, 1996).

Slavery and the birth of white privilege

The idea that people who look different *are*, in some way, profoundly different was instrumental in racialising slavery. Until the invention of race, those who worked in the plantations and grand houses of the Caribbean and the USA were mainly from Ireland, Africa and Scotland. Some were indentured labourers, who, in theory at least, were free to leave once they had worked off their debt, and some were slaves. As rebellion fomented amongst the workers, the plantation owners adopted a divide and rule policy. The plantation owners cast the Africans as different, as inferior – and the other workers as superior because they belonged to the new legal category of 'white'. White people could no longer be enslaved. Only Africans could be slaves.

The white workers on the plantations went up a rung as an even lower rung was put beneath them. They were given small privileges, positions of authority, and were encouraged to see themselves as superior – to stop identifying with the Africans with whom they worked and to identify instead with the white landowners for whom they all worked. White privilege came into being as some workers gained status simply because they were white. The African workers on the other hand lost what few rights they had ever had, including any eventual hope of freedom, either for themselves or their children. By the mid-eighteenth century the idea that all black people, whether a slave or not, were inferior to all other races had taken hold.

Alliances changed as indentured workers identified as white rather than as exploited. The plantation owners, whose huge economic advantage had been built on the backs of these indentured workers, quietened rebellion by dividing white from black. The economic privilege was still with the plantation owners – there was no economic or social equality built into this new concept of 'white'. The only privilege that the white workers actually had was the belief that they were superior to black people, and the authority to express this belief with violence. The plantation owners had consolidated their power by creating a middle management to enforce obedience.

> ## Modern Slavery
>
> Slavery and indentured labour is still very much a part of the world's economy. There are more slaves today than ever before – over 40 million (Global Slavery Index, 2019). Enslaved labour still picks our cotton (cotton production almost always involves slavery at some point). Enslaved children mine the minerals used in our electronic devices (and the profits are often used to fund civil wars). It is, if you live in Britain, entirely possible that you've eaten eggs collected by a slave, particularly if it was a 'Happy' egg, or, even more ironically, a 'Freedom' egg (Lawrence, 2016). Nail bars, car washes, construction, agriculture, food processing, the sex trade and the care industry are all frequent exploiters of slaves (Anti-Slavery, 2019).
>
> Will Kerr, the director of the National Crime Agency says that the number of modern-day slaves in the UK (including indentured workers) is likely to be tens of thousands and that, in contemporary Britain, many of us are likely to come into contact with someone who is enslaved (Lawrence, 2016). As counsellors we should be particularly good at noticing if someone seems fearful, depressed, submissive and withdrawn. Of course, this does not necessarily indicate that they are being kept against their will, but if the person also allows someone else to speak for them, if they avoid making eye contact, look unkempt, malnourished and/or show signs of physical restraint or injury, your suspicions should be aroused. It is easy to do something if you suspect that someone is being forced to work against their will. Just go to www.modernslaveryhelpline.org/report and fill in a form. It doesn't take long and you don't have to give your name if you don't want to.
>
> However, helping, or trying to help, always happens within a larger context. Before taking any action, it may be wise to find out how the Home Office is currently treating those who have been enslaved. This has, recently, been very badly (Bulman, 2019a, 2019b). The help that we can give another, whether in therapy or in another context, is limited, or even sabotaged, if the larger environment is hostile. Addressing this hostility by supporting campaigns (to, for instance, not send freed slaves back into the hands of gang masters) or taking other forms of political action that help make the environment less hostile is an appropriate and necessary aspect of therapeutic work.

Race and psychology

Once in the blood, race entered the heart and mind. As skulls were measured, theories were constructed about the relative innate intelligence and morality of the different races. Race became a matter of psychology as well as biology,

Blumenbach concluding that 'negroes' were intelligent and intellectually sophisticated (Blumenbach, 1865) and that differences in skull shape could be explained by cultural practices such as swaddling babies to a board. This aspect of his thought was discarded, whilst his research measuring skulls was foundational to developing race theory and still provides the racial categorisations we use today.

The idea that race is biological became the idea that racial differences are genetic. The Eugenics Movement facilitated the development of this idea from the 1880s onwards. The Eugenic agenda aimed to preserve 'purity' of 'blood' and so give 'the more suitable races or strains of blood a better chance of prevailing over the less suitable' (Galton, 1883). It was also concerned with intra-racial purity, and so 30,000 people who were considered defective in some way were sterilised in the US. The Holocaust took Eugenics a step further. Jews were legally defined by 'blood' in the 1935 Nuremberg Laws, as were Roma and Poles and 'Asiatic' peoples of the Soviet Union, who were killed in vast numbers during the Holocaust – along with disabled people, gay people, inter-sex and transgender people, political prisoners and Jehovah's Witnesses (who refused to swear an oath to the regime or perform military service).

Although deeply unfashionable after the Holocaust, this determination to prove that intelligence is determined by race persisted into the twentieth century, with the publication of psychologist Richard Herrnstein and the political scientist Charles Murray's *The Bell Curve: Intelligence and Class Structure in American Life* in 1994. Herrnstein and Murray argue not only that intelligence is affected by race, but that since intelligence is (in their view) inherent, any efforts to improve educational opportunities for those not doing so well is a waste of resources, a claim robustly debunked by a host of social and political theorists.

The uses and abuses of research

There is a complex relationship between research and the society in which it is produced and used. The early European naturalists generally got their data not from direct contact with the people they were studying, but from those involved in the slave trade – and those naturalists were instrumental in sustaining that trade. These researchers varied in the theories they set forth and in the degree of hostility they expressed towards other peoples. Some of them held other peoples in high esteem, yet their work was instrumental in developing the foundation of racism – the idea of racial difference.

Darwinism is a particularly telling example of the relationship between scientific theory and the time and place in which it is produced and consumed. Darwin's biographers, Desmond and Moore (1991) suggest that his work was heavily influenced by his strongly abolitionist background and by his horror of what he had seen of the aftermath of a slave rebellion while voyaging on *The Beagle*. The attitudes that Darwin brought to his scientific work were, I imagine, also influenced by his having had a black teacher. John Edmonstone taught taxidermy at the University of Edinburgh – and was a freed slave. Taxidermy, which proved to be an indispensable skill in his later research, was not a part of Darwin's medical studies at Edinburgh, but he had the foresight to arrange private lessons with

Edmonstone, who lived a few doors away. Darwin says that they spent many hours in conversation and that he considered Edmonstone, whom he describes as intelligent and very pleasant, a close friend.

Darwin's *The Origin of Species* argues that all human beings have a common origin, yet by the late 1860s, his theory of evolution was being used to support the idea that we have *different* origins (Stephan, 1982). Darwin responded by using *The Descent of Man* to argue that all human beings have one common human origin. The biological similarities between the different races were, he said, too great for the idea that we have different origins to be plausible; and the physical characteristics used to define race were superficial, and not due to evolution. There is no sudden lightening or darkening of skin tone as one moves across the globe. It is gradual. Darwin thought human variation to be so diverse that it would be impossible to ever fully systemise it – and that there was little point trying to do so as it is not of any scientific significance.

However, Social Darwinists transposed Darwin's theory of biological evolution onto the social world and in doing so replaced the old divinely ordained racial hierarchy with one that sounded scientific (but isn't). It was not Darwin, but the Social Darwinist Herbert Spencer who, in 1874, first coined the phrase 'survival of the fittest'. He suggested that human societies operate according to the principles of natural selection just like biological species. He saw racial conflict as the key to social progress because, as he saw it, conflict allowed the more powerful to overwhelm and drive out those less powerful (Greene, 1963).

I said, in a previous publication (Tolan with Cameron, 2017), that science did not discover race – it invented it. This is an over-simplification. Science serves, and is served by multiple political, economic and social agendas. The relationships are complex. Science is both misused and misunderstood. The relationship between race and medical science is currently entering a new chapter. The outcome is yet to be decided.

Race is still not biological

Having shied away from race for several decades after the Holocaust, science has finally announced that race is *not* biological. The first human genome researchers stood with President Clinton as he announced, in 2000, there is no biological foundation to race. The message was clear and decisive. It is, then, potentially confusing that race is now at the top of genome researchers' agenda. This has happened for two reasons. Firstly, genome researchers have identified 'clusters' of genomic similarity that relate to geographical areas, and they are looking for a term to use for them. Some researchers think that 'race' is as good a term as any. When race theory started out, the term 'race' was used synonymously with 'type', and this is the usage that these scientists are using when trying to re-introduce the term. Others feel that using the term 'race' in this way is not only confusing, but that it sweeps the history and social legacy of race theory under the carpet.

The second reason that the term 'race' is being used in genomic research is that genome researchers are in a very good position to tackle racial inequalities in health – and are very keen to do so. Race is not a scientific reality, but science was instrumental in making it a social reality. Race may be a scientific fiction but it is very real in the sense that it impacts what sort of housing you are likely to live in, how likely you are to be taken into care as a child, your experience of education, how you are treated by the police and the courts, the kinds of jobs you might be welcomed into (or not), how likely you are to be given a psychiatric diagnosis and how long you're likely to live.

Race also affects what you are likely to die of. This is partly because the genetic mutations that cause particular diseases, or a vulnerability to particular diseases, are acquired through genetic inheritance. 'We all inherit some genetic variations from one or both parents, and if a relatively small population of people, with all their genetic variations, gets separated from other populations, they'll pass down those variations to their descendants. Eventually, those particular variations become more common in that particular population and particular diseases become more common in particular populations' (Cameron, 2017: 130). This is different to biological race theory. Genomic research does *not* support the idea that the members of any particular race share some biological feature that makes them alike and different to the members of other races – or that some races are superior to others. There are many different genetically significant 'clusters' within continental populations and within perceived racial groups.

People in different parts of the world get different diseases, not because they are of different races, but because they come from particular geographical regions. Sickness does not recognise race. Sickle cell anaemia is commonly thought of as a disease that only affects black people. It isn't. It also affects people from Central and South America, the Middle East, Asia and the Mediterranean. Nor does it potentially affect all black people. The sickle cell trait is an immune response to malaria and so shows up most frequently in people from, or descended from, malarial regions of Africa – or Central and South America, the Middle East, Asia and the Mediterranean.

Science now has the potential to stop some of the harm caused by the legacy of scientific race theory. However, in order to begin doing so, genome research has had to address some unintended racism. Having proved once and for all that race is not biological, the early genomic researchers ignored race and did not make a point of including black or Asian people in their research. The unintended result of this was that they knew far more about the diseases Europeans tend to suffer from, but rather little about anyone else. Genome research has now moved from being a 'race-free' science to being what the sociologist Catherine Bliss (2015) calls a 'race-positive' science and is trying to even up the playing field by understanding more about the kinds of genetic variations carried by people from other continents, and their descendants.

This re-pairing of race and genetics has mutated a little as it has been taken into public consciousness. Race seems to be back, but it is as illusory as ever. DNA testing companies can't tell you what your racial heritage is. They can tell you who you are related to now. They do this by comparing markers in your genes to markers from those other people around the world that are in their databases. Your 'ancestry' is decided on the basis of who you share DNA with now, not a century ago. Forensic anthropologists don't know what race the murder victim was, only what part of the world their ancestors came from. They then deduce the race that the victim would likely have been, if race was real (they are well aware it is not, see Sauer, 1992). Many people use inverted commas when writing about 'race' to indicate that they are aware that it is not a scientific reality, and I will do this in the rest of this book.

Although the whole notion of 'race' is a fiction, it is a fiction that has been accepted by so many for so long, that it has become a fact. The *idea* that there are 'races' of people who are in some way biologically alike and different from other 'races' has created a *social* reality. 'Race' was invented – and now it is real. Another way of saying this is that race is not real, but racism is. We fail racially marginalised clients if we allow ourselves to be ignorant, or downplay the realities of life in a hostile environment. We also fail racially marginalised colleagues.

The notion of 'race' ensnares us in paradox. 'Race' is not scientifically real, yet the *idea* that it is, in itself, created something that *is* real and affects all aspects of life for all people in racialised societies. Those lower down the racial hierarchy are made aware of this on a daily basis. Those at the top may glide through an entire lifetime without ever being aware of how their 'race' shapes their life, but it does. Chapter 9 discusses this in more detail.

> **Reflective exercise**
>
> Depending on whether you are working alone or with others, think, write or talk about how you became aware that people are categorised according to 'race' and how you became aware of your own racial identity. Who talked to you about 'race' and what ideas about 'race' were communicated to you?

Ethnicity

'Race' and ethnicity are not the same – you can be beaten up one day because you are black, and beaten up the next day because you are Tutsi or Karo (this happens, especially when asylum seekers are rehoused without any thought as to who they have fled from). Although it is often used to do so, ethnicity should not imply 'race' (in the sense of someone looking or sounding 'ethnic'). We're all ethnic. We all have at least one mother tongue, land, history, mythology and traditions that we identify with.

These identifications constitute ethnicity in everyone, but tend to be used only when making people 'other'. The term 'ethnic' was, for instance, used in the early twentieth century to make the refugees arriving in the USA from Eastern Europe and the Mediterranean different to the existing white population. 'Ethnic' is still mostly used in the process of presenting some groups of people as different, although the term 'minority ethnic' rather than 'ethnic minority' is used in an attempt to counter this and emphasise that everyone is ethnic.

Ethnicity is clearly a social construction rather than a biological reality. Our genes do not make us speak a particular language or like a particular kind of food; our tastes, values and the way we express ourselves result from the ways in which we are socialised.

However, ethnicity is also a social construction in a more abstract way. The term 'ethnic group' originates in anthropology, and contemporary anthropologists are realising that some so-called 'ethnic groups' may have been identified in a way that does not match how they themselves identify. In these instances, ethnicity is an imposition – the kind of imposition that attacks a person or a people's sense of themselves. It might be wise to remember that the box your client ticks on your agency's equality monitoring form may not match your client's actual ethnic identity.

> **Self-awareness exercise**
>
> Depending on whether you are working alone or with others, think, write or talk about how aware you are of your ethnicity, and why. Do you think that other people identify your ethnicity in the way that you do? What feelings do your answers provoke?

Nationality and nationality status

Although ethnic groups are usually associated with a particular place, ethnicity is not the same as nationality. Yoruba is an ethnicity and Yoruba people live in Nigeria – and Benin, Toga, Ghana, Sierra Leone and Ivory Coast. Nationality can be used as an identity – one can be proud or ashamed to be British, for example – but nationality is essentially a legal relationship in which a country takes responsibility for your safety and assumes authority over you.

Like 'race' and ethnicity, nationality as an identity can be used to 'other' – one may hate Germans, or the French – and often is used in this way when relations between countries are hostile. However, it is nationality as a legal status that is the current focus of difference-making throughout the economically privileged countries of the world. People so desperate that they risk their lives and endure horrendous conditions in the hope of living in a safer country are denied basic human rights like dignity, fairness, equality and respect before they can even ask for legal rights. Those denied the legal right to protection are forced to choose between destitution or returning to whatever they had fled from. This denial of human rights is the most fundamental form of making someone 'different'. Denial of basic human rights is a denial of someone's humanity.

> **Case study**
>
> Khalid, who had been smuggled out of his home country and had arrived in the UK as an unaccompanied child, had been seeing Leila, a counsellor at his school, for three years. Khalid still had nightmares about his family's home being searched and his father being found and then taken away. He was extremely anxious in situations in which he was not in control. Leila was aware that Susan, his social worker, was being careful not to inflame his anxiety in relation to the asylum claim that she was helping him make to secure his right to stay in the UK once he had turned 18. Leila tried to support Susan's efforts by taking a 'there's no point worrying about what hasn't happened yet' approach. This helped Leila manage her own anxiety, but was of little help to Khalid, whose claim was denied and who was forced to return to a still simmering country with which he no longer had any ties.

Religion

Nor are ethnicity and religion the same – usually. The Bantu, for example, are Muslim in Somalia and Christian in Kenya, and lots of different ethnic groups identify as Muslim, or Christian, the world over. But sometimes ethnicity and religion are not separable. I missed both when working, for just one session, with a young Iraqi woman. She was so full of what she had to bring that it was not appropriate to ask her about her background, but I was curious. I have spent a lot of time with Muslim friends in different contexts and I am (I think) fairly well attuned to cues that announce a Muslim identity. I was struck by their absence. It was not until I saw the chilling news footage of the Yazidi stranded on a mountaintop in Iraq (Chulov, 2014) that I realised that she may have had an ethnic and religious identity with which I was not familiar. Because religion is conflated with ethnicity, and ethnicity with race, religion and race are also often conflated – as many Sikhs, Hindus and Thomasine Christians have found in the current Islamophobic climate.

Conclusion

'Race' is a social experience, rather than a biological fact – but it, or rather racism, is only too real. Using 'ethnicity' as a euphemism for 'race' denies this reality. Racism is about 'race'. Many people also face hostility on account of their ethnicity, their nationality, their religion and/or their nationality status. It is important to recognise that a client may face hostility from several intersecting directions (there is more about 'intersectionality' in Chapter 5) and to properly acknowledge each when appropriate.

Further reading

Akala (2018) *Natives: Race and Class in the Ruins of Empire*. London: Hodder & Stoughton.
McGarry, A. (2017) *Romaphobia: The Last Acceptable Form of Racism*. London: Zed Books.
Morning, A. (2014) 'And you thought we had moved beyond all that: Biological race returns to the social sciences', *Ethnic and Racial Studies*, 37(10): 1676–85.

3
The Social Construction of Difference: Gender, Sex, Sexuality, Disability, Age and Class

'I don't like people like you.
You're different to me'

Learning aims

- To understand how 'difference' is constructed through gender, sex, sexuality, disability, age and class. This provides a conceptual base with which to understand some of the ideas discussed in later chapters and also a cognitive basis from which to begin changing your prejudices and biases.
- To appreciate that the politics of inclusion and exclusion is inherent in all social identities.
- To think, via reflective exercises and case studies, about the practice implications of the social construction of various 'differences'.
- To cultivate critical professional awareness by understanding how our professional ancestors contributed to the creation of pathologised sexual identities.

Gender: A disputed idea

And what of the 'natural' difference between the sexes? Much has been made, in the past, of a woman's childbearing capacity making her 'naturally' unfit for public life. Once more effective contraception became widely available, those who stepped in to guard the innate distinction between men and women's psychological differences have sought to prove that women's brains are from Venus and men's from Mars.

Meanwhile in the social sciences, the idea that men and women might both be from planet Earth was helped by a distinction between sex (male and female) and gender (masculine and feminine). One of the originators of this distinction was the anthropologist Margaret Mead, who, in 1928, published the results of her research with three societies in New Guinea. Mead found quite extreme variations in women and men's temperaments in these different societies. Although she did not use the word 'gender', Mead did use the concept in concluding that differences between the temperament of women and the temperament of men could not be due to innate differences arising from their different reproductive functions. Generations of feminists have since argued that gender cannot, therefore, be considered to be biologically determined.

The idea that gender is acquired through social learning rather than being biologically innate was popularised in the 1970s and 1980s. Following on from Simone de Beauvoir's (1949) observation that 'one is not born a woman, one becomes one', feminists began to argue that we are, from the moment of birth, taught how to be men (i.e. masculine) or how to be women (i.e. feminine). These days little girls and little boys are (sometimes) less likely to be dressed in pink or blue, and many boys are encouraged to express their feelings and girls to 'be strong'. However, although some of the messages society gives us about what is gender appropriate have changed a little (and only for some), they have not stopped.

Every society constructs differences between men and women, and constructs similarities amongst men and amongst women. Women and men are given different social roles and responsibilities on this basis and these gender roles come with particular expectations. Women and men therefore have different life experiences, ambitions, desires, motivations and feelings arising out of these different life experiences – we become, as de Beauvoir says, a woman (or a man).

Rather than become mired in the debate as to whether 'feminine' traits are innate or learned, some feminists took ownership of aspects of 'femininity'. This position argues that men and women are indeed different, and that the way women are should be valued no less than the way men are. Carol Gilligan's research, for example, showed that, when faced with an abstract ethical problem, women generally wanted more information about the context and the people involved, how they felt and how they related to each other, whereas men, generally, did not. Her point is that a concern for people is as valid a foundation as a concern for principles when considering ethical problems. Her work is regarded as sparking the development of relational ethics, a perspective that many therapists use when resolving ethical problems, whether they are familiar with the term or not.

> **Reflective exercise**
>
> Mead showed that notions of femininity and masculinity differ in relation to ethnicity. They also differ in relation to other social institutions such as age and class. Working-class women, for example, were never expected to be wilting violets.
>
> Map the different ideas about femininity and masculinity that you grew up with. Are they different for the younger people in your life?
>
> Think about some or all of your clients. Do you imagine that they were brought up with similar or different ideas about femininity and masculinity? How well do you think you understand those different ideas?
>
> The sticking together of biological sex with gender excludes those who are not cisgendered and whose gender identity does not match the gender identity ascribed to them on the basis of their biological sex. This includes people who:
>
> - feel so strongly masculine or feminine that they feel that they have been born in the wrong body. Some may experience bodily dysphoria, the sense that their body has the wrong sexual organs, and some do not
> - people who do not experience themselves as having a gender at all
> - people who feel like a man some of the time and a women at other times
> - many other variations in self-experience.

Until very recently people who do not conform to the gender assigned to their biological sex have usually, in the global north (regions that are economically privileged in comparison to those in the global south), felt unable to live in a way that is congruent with their identity.

The philosopher Judith Butler suggests that rather than seeing gender as something that we *are*, or as something that we *become* (through social learning), we instead understand gender as something that we *do*. In saying that gender is 'performative', Butler refers to the ways in which we enact (or resist) gender conventions by moving and talking in particular ways or choosing certain kinds of clothing, etc. In saying that gender is 'performative' rather than that gender is 'a performance', Butler makes a distinction between gender as something that we choose, in the sense of consciously acting in a feminine or masculine way (performance), and unconsciously imitating an abstract ideal of femininity or masculinity (performativity) (Williams, C., 2014). The arguments that gender is performative – or socially constructed – are sometimes misunderstood as claiming that gender, and therefore gender identities, are not real. The previous chapter illustrated the paradoxical reality of race. Similarly, there need be no biological basis to gender in order for many, both cisgendered and otherwise, to feel painfully constrained by the gender roles imposed upon them.

> **Self-awareness exercise**
>
> How do you perform gender? How do you dress, style your hair, walk, talk? Are there any ways in which you are a gender rebel? Would you like to be?

Sex

Not only are masculinity and femininity constructed by society, but so too is the idea that bodies are unambiguously either male or female. One in 1500 or 2000 babies are not, at birth, clearly male or female (this is around the same proportion as people with green eyes). More are born with subtler sex variations, some of which do not become evident until later in life.

The United Nations says that:

> intersex people are born with sex characteristics (including genitals, gonads and chromosome patterns) that do not fit typical binary notions of male or female bodies. Intersex is an umbrella term used to describe a wide range of natural bodily variations. In some cases, intersex traits are visible at birth while in others, they are not apparent until puberty. Some chromosomal intersex variations may not be physically apparent at all. (United Nations, 2015)

In Europe, the demand that intersex people live as either a man or a woman began in the Middle Ages, and the punishment for not doing so was often death. More recently, the social construction of sex has been enforced by medicine. Estimates of how many people are intersex vary between .05 to 1.7 per cent of the population, depending upon the definition used (Blackless et al., 2000). Babies are usually started on a lengthy regime of 'corrective' surgery and hormonal 'treatment' immediately after birth. This is done in the belief that the child will not be able to live comfortably in society unless they fit its norms. In other words it is done for cultural rather than medical reasons.

Sexuality

Sex and gender are sometimes confused with sexuality (or as it is now less commonly called, sexual orientation). Strictly speaking, 'sexuality' should refer to a wider category of what arouses you (and 'sexual orientation' to who arouses you) but it is usually used to make a distinction only between gay and straight.

The question of whether sexuality is innate – whether there is a 'gay gene' – has its own particular history of political significance largely thanks to those who have used – and may still use – conversion 'therapies' that aim to make gay people straight. Contemporary conversion therapy (usually) consists of talking therapy, but techniques used in the global north in the (recent) past have included lobotomies, hormonal treatment or 'chemical castration', and giving a client nausea-inducing drugs or electric shocks to their genitals while they are required to watch gay porn.

Homosexuality was removed from the American *Diagnostic and Statistical Manual* (DSM) in 1973 after gay and lesbian activists disrupted annual meetings of the American Psychiatric Association. The Association was willing to listen. Gay activists explained the stigma caused by the pathologisation of homosexuality to the Association's next annual meeting and the following year a gay psychiatrist talked (anonymously) about the discrimination he faced within the profession. Institutional and individual professional responsibility involves being willing to listen when we are being told that what we are doing is harmful. It also involves being willing to call out harmful beliefs and practices when we ourselves see them.

However, although homosexuality was removed as a diagnosis, it was replaced, in DSM II, by a new diagnosis, 'Sexual Orientation Disturbance' (yes, the acronym is SOD), which allowed homosexuality to still be regarded as an illness if an individual found their same-sex attraction disturbing. This legitimised the practice of sexual conversion therapies. The diagnosis of SOD was replaced, in DSM III, by 'Ego Dystonic Homosexuality' before the American Psychiatric Association eventually concluded, in 1987, that neither was actually an illness.

Statements by professional organisations on conversion therapy

www.bacp.co.uk/docs/pdf/15512_ethical%20framework%202013.pdf

www.psychotherapy.org.uk/wp-content/uploads/2016/09/Memorandum-of-understanding-on-conversion-therapy.pdf

www.bps.org.uk/system/files/Public%20files/conversion_therapy_final_version.pdf

www.apa.org/pi/lgbt/resources/therapeutic-response.pdf

The mental health professions have not only been complicit in the persecution of gay people, but also, according to the influential French sociologist Michel Foucault, instrumental in the invention of 'the homosexual'. Prior to sex becoming an object of scientific study during the Victorian era, sexual policing was about *what* you fancied. Once sexologists got involved, it became about *who* you fancied. People have always had sex with same-sex partners, but had not thought of themselves – and were not thought of – as homosexual.

Foucault refused to have anything to with the question of whether or not sexuality is innate. The question he was interested in was how sexuality came to be about identity. In showing how the *idea* of sexuality was constructed, Foucault makes a distinction between a concern (in ancient Rome, China, Japan, India, and the Arabic-Muslim world) with erotic pleasure (which he called *ars erotica* or erotic arts) and the Victorian construction of a science of sexuality (which he called *scientia sexualis*).

In the *ars erotica* secrets are passed from expert to novice in the quest for pleasure. In *scientia sexualis*, secrets are confessed, firstly by sinners in search of redemption (some sexual acts, and all sexual acts in some circumstances were/are seen as sinful), then by research subjects, and then by patients and clients in search of their 'true selves'. Foucault identifies five ways in which confession and science were brought together. They may be familiar to you:

- hypnosis, and free association
- understanding sexual desire as the cause and explanation of all sorts of behaviour
- understanding sexuality as something hidden
- making the response of the listener essential
- seeing confession as therapeutic.

Confession is, Foucault says, a means by which we are controlled, but it has become such an important and commonplace aspect of our lives that we no longer think of it as a means by which we are controlled; rather, we think of it as a path to liberation.

> **Reflective exercise**
>
> Depending on whether you are working alone or with others, think, write or talk about:
>
> What, if anything, your theoretical approach has to say about homosexuality.
>
> What are your own beliefs about sexual preferences? How do these beliefs impact your work with clients?
>
> Whether you need to find a way of reconciling your professional and personal beliefs.

Disability

Disability is another difference that has been made to seem like the work of nature. The old understanding of disability as the wages of sin, or as one's cross to bear, has given way to seeing disability as a medical concern. The medical *understanding* of physical and cognitive impairments is, of course, important. However, the medical *construction* of disability reduces people to their medical condition, and predisposes us to see (or wonder about) a person's medical condition before we see them as a person.

The problem with the medical model is that it understands disabled people as being in relationship with the medical professions rather than with the whole community. The social model, on the other hand, sees people being disabled by an inaccessible or otherwise alienating environment. Academic Disability Studies and the Disability Rights Movement use the term 'impairment' to identify a physical or cognitive difference, and 'disabled' to identify a common experience of social exclusion.

Historically, disabled people have been excluded within – then from – their communities. Those taken away, for life, to huge institutions were disabled not by their impairment but by being denied a family life, a proper education, rewarding work, a social life and a sexual life (and were often abused, sexually, financially, emotionally and physically). Most of these institutions are gone, and those who had been sent away have returned to their communities – only to once again be excluded. Disabled people are still excluded by buildings that ought to be accessible but are not, by braille and signing still being the exception rather than the rule, by discrimination in the workplace, a lack of support funding for schools and by the hostility of strangers.

The Deaf community has a particularly strong group identity as people who share a visual and kinaesthetic rather than a hearing perception of the world. A capital 'D' signifies Deafness as cultural, social and linguistic group identification: 'd/D' is often used as an inclusive way of referring to deaf people who do not particularly identify with Deaf culture as well as those who do.

Reflective exercise

Is the room that you work in wheelchair accessible? Is it accessible to clients with other mobility issues? Do you know how to access an interpreter for d/Deaf clients? (Chapter 10 tells you how.)

Depending on whether you are working alone or with others, think, write or talk about how you feel about making the effort to be more accessible.

Age

Nature does not even determine whether you are young or old. That too is determined by social forces. Being young and being old are, at different times and places, marginalised identities. Like gender, age is thought of differently in different societies. Age is, like race, gender, sex and sexuality a social construction, a way of arranging social relationships.

Case study

Zee was a 33-year-old woman, originally from a country in the global south, who worked in fashion and had a rather glamorous job. She often complained about being old. The first few times she did this, I heard what she said in the context of her working in such a youth-oriented industry. I was taken aback to realise that she not only thought of herself as an old person but that she *experienced* herself as old. Her joints ached, she was easily tired and she saw her health as inevitably deteriorating in the near future.

Childhood, adulthood and old age look, sound and feel very different depending on where you are and when you're there – or, sometimes where your parents are from, and when they left.

Case study

When my client Fahad's parents came to Britain from Bangladesh in the 1970s, his dad was 15, his mother 14, and they already had two children. I understood that adulthood had began much earlier for Fahad's parents than is usual in Britain, and it was from this context that I was able to appreciate the humour silently shared by Fahad and his mother when she pretended not to know that he had his own car (Fahad was, at 14, a successful entrepreneur outside school hours). She knew, Fahad said, that he shouldn't really be driving, and then made a gesture that gave me to understand that she also thought that since she'd, at 14, been old enough to look after him, he was old enough to run some errands for her on his suspiciously speedy trips around London. Thankfully, Fahad was 19 when he told me this and had never had an accident while driving illegally (nor had he physically harmed anyone in the course of his business activities). I suspect that, had I been seeing him when he was 15, Fahad might have taken my cultural understanding of age into account and not allowed me to guess that he drove.

Reflective exercise

Depending on whether you are working alone or with others, think, write or talk about your own beliefs, values and expectations around:

Childhood
Adulthood
Old age

Pick a client or several clients whose background is different to your own in some way, and depending on whether you are working alone or with others, think, write or talk about whether you think that there are differences in the way you construct childhood, adulthood or old age and if there are, how do you think that this impacts the therapy?

Class

Beverley Skeggs (1997), whose work was discussed in the previous chapter, is one of several contemporary class researchers who argue that working-class women do not want to identify as such because they feel so stigmatised by the way working-class women are portrayed in the media. Recent research (Savage et al., 2013) into class identity reveals that although aware of class as a political reality, many people do not readily identify as middle or working class.

The Marxist distinction of class by occupation no longer works as well as it once did. The sociologist Pierre Bourdieu (1986) suggests that we understand class not by occupation – you're middle class if you're a teacher and working class if you're a builder, etc. – but in terms of access and exclusion. Inclusion depends upon 'economic capital' (what you have – property, earnings, savings, etc.), 'social capital' (who you know) and 'cultural capital' (your taste, which is largely set by education and upbringing). Bourdieu considered cultural capital to be essential in acquiring social and economic capital. In other words, social mobility depends on reading the right books, liking the right kind of music, etc., and this depends upon what sort of influences you grew up with at home and at school.

Cultural capital must be given credibility through symbolic capital. Symbolic capital affirms taste, and like other forms of capital, it is not evenly distributed. The Burberry brand camel, white and black plaid had a great deal of symbolic capital when it was associated with upper middle-class shoppers, but its value plummeted when it became thought of as 'chavvy'. Taste is the new snobbery that keeps some people as outsiders, regardless of how rich and well connected they are. Imogen Tyler and Bruce Bennett's (2010) study of celebrity culture shows how women such as the 'wag' Coleen Rooney are vilified as 'chavvy' despite having access to a lot of money (economic capital) and to other rich people (social capital). Class still matters, but it is implicit in social relationships rather than necessarily being the means by which people tend to identify themselves.

Mike Savage (2013), who, along with colleagues, conducted The Great British Class Survey in 2011 (you might have seen it presented on television, although it got rather less coverage than *The Great British Bake Off*), proposes seven classes, rather than the usual three. These are:

The elite, who have the highest levels of economic, social and cultural capital and whose economic wealth sets them apart from the rest of the population. They are a small, exclusive class, concentrated in the south east of England, have the lowest proportion of racial minorities and the highest proportion of graduates.

The established middle class are comfortably well off and often work in management or the professions. They have a higher proportion of racial minorities than the elite and have the highest social capital of all the classes. They engage with both highbrow culture (e.g. opera) and 'emerging' cultural capital (social media, going to the gym, going to gigs). They have a high proportion of graduates.

The technical middle class is quite small – only 6 per cent of the national population – and, despite the stereotype of nerdy men, has a slightly higher than average number of women. This class is relatively prosperous, but less likely to be graduates, professionals or managers. Their network of friends and contacts is very restricted, although their contacts tend to be high status. They are not particularly engaged with either highbrow or emerging cultural capital.

New affluent workers live in a relatively costly home, have a moderate income, a small amount of savings, and are economically secure without being very well off. There is a high proportion of young people and 57 per cent are men. They tend to live in the old manufacturing centres outside the south east of England. They engage with emerging cultural capital more than highbrow cultural capital and have the second highest social capital. They tend to come from non-middle-class families, and have achieved their relative security without significant inherited economic or cultural capital. Relatively few have been to university, and those who have tend to be graduates of the new universities. They form a significant part of the population – 15 per cent – and cannot easily be identified as either middle or working class. They are a complex and unusually fluid grouping.

The traditional working class typically own their homes, and have modest savings, but are low on nearly every measure of capital, particularly emerging cultural capital. Their social networks are quite restricted and few are graduates. A disproportionate number are women – more than any other class. They tend to live in old industrial areas outside the south east of England, especially in Scotland, Wales and Northern Ireland.

Emergent service workers typically have a modest household income, limited savings and are likely to rent. They have a relatively high number of social contacts and their emerging cultural capital is higher than for any other class, but their highbrow cultural capital is low. Most are relatively young, with an average age of 34, and a unusually high proportion are racial minorities. They tend to work in relatively insecure service jobs in catering, customer services and call centres.

The precariat are the poorest class economically and also have very low levels of social and cultural capital. Their household income is low, their savings negligible, and they are likely to rent in old industrial areas, but often away from the major cities. They are unlikely to be graduates and may be unemployed or working in badly paid, insecure jobs. They form a relatively large class – 15 per cent of the population.

Poverty

Poverty is often associated with being working class, but the two do not necessarily go together. Working-class people are usually (but not always) comparatively poor in relation to the wealthier middle and upper classes, but do not necessarily see themselves as poor if they have more than enough to live on (just as middle-class people do not generally consider themselves poor although they are comparatively poor in relation to the elite).

Not having enough to live on used to be comparatively rare in Britain, but is now commonplace. Food-banks have come into existence. So have the working poor. Homelessness, both rough sleeping and hidden in hostels, B&Bs and sofa surfing, has been forced upon a staggering number of people. Being homeless is currently one of our brutally stigmatised identities, with homeless people regularly ignored, dismissed, beaten-up, urinated upon and set on fire.

The cumulative effects of a governmental policy of austerity have led to unprecedented numbers of people, both working and middle class, being without a financial cushion to shield them from the economic consequences of life events. The gig economy is insecure and badly paid with no sickness, maternity or holiday pay. Those who fall on hard times are treated with contempt by the profit-making agencies contracted to provide basic services. Poverty is both normalised and stigmatised.

Poverty is the most pressing issue for many disabled people. Those who are transgender experience disproportionate poverty. Many in the 'squeezed middle', whose class privileges previously protected them from economic insecurity, have experienced relative poverty for the first time. Poverty is exhausting, demoralising and degrading. It is important that as therapists we are able to recognise its presence, even in unexpected places.

Conclusion

The social constructionist view advanced in this chapter holds that although our lives are very different depending on our 'race', ethnicity, gender, sex, sexuality and whether we are disabled, we are not, in essence, different. There are no innate racial differences that make members of a particular 'race' alike and different to people of other 'races'. Ethnic and class differences are cultural and changeable. People are disabled by a rejecting environment rather than by their own bodies. We've not always felt the need to identify ourselves in terms of our sexual preferences. Not everybody is unambiguously either male or female, and not all females feminine or all males masculine. We are one human race – and we're all from the same planet.

Although we are not as different as some like to imagine, we are more diverse than is commonly acknowledged. Some people, simply by being, resist easy identification on the basis of 'race', gender, sex, sexual orientation or disability. They are the invisible 'others', the disappeared, denied existence by a category.

Our differences may be artefact rather than scientific fact, but they are real enough to have created, and to maintain, multiple social, economic and political inequalities. All our lives would be very different if the idea of 'race' had not been used to facilitate the exploitation of millions of people. Your – and my – economic situation would be different, the world map would be different and our histories would be different. We would think of ourselves very differently if gender were not so entwined with sex. We might think of our community spaces very differently had disabled people not been taken away from their families and communities for so long. Our family histories would have been very different had generations of gay relatives not been obliged to take cover. The understanding of some people as innately different – the construction of 'them' and 'us' – is embedded in our experience of community life and our experience of ourselves. This is as true of therapists as it is of clients and calls for an awareness of where we sit within social hierarchies as well as a desire to understand diverse life experiences. 'Reflexivity' is a concept that refers to an awareness of one's social positions. It differs from self-reflection in that it is concerned with the socio-political rather than the psychological. It is more often used in research than in therapy but is essential in both.

Further reading

Gender

Boswell, H. (2013) 'The transgender paradigm shift towards free expression', in T. Ore (ed.), *The Social Construction of Difference and Inequality: Race, Class, Gender, and Sexuality*, 6th edn. New York: McGraw-Hill. pp. 114–18.

Lorber, J. (1993) 'Believing is seeing: Biology as ideology', *Gender and Society*, 7(4): 568–81.

Lorber, J. (2013) 'The social construction of gender', in T. Ore (ed.), *The Social Construction of Difference and Inequality: Race, Class, Gender, and Sexuality*, 6th edn. New York: McGraw-Hill. pp. 112–20.

Intersex

King, B.W. (2016) 'Becoming the intelligible other: Speaking intersex bodies against the grain', *Critical Discourse Studies*, 13(4): 359–78.

Kleeman, J. (2016) '"We don't know if your baby's a boy or a girl": Growing up intersex', *The Guardian*, 2 July. Available at: www.theguardian.com/world/2016/jul/02/male-and-female-what-is-it-like-to-be-intersex (accessed 10 September 2019).

Sexuality

Broido, E. (1999) 'Constructing identity: The nature and meaning of lesbian, gay, and bisexual identities', in M. Perez, K.A. DeBord and K.J. Bieschke (eds), *Handbook of Counseling and Psychotherapy with Lesbian, Gay, and Bisexual Clients*. Washington, DC: American Psychological Association.

This article contains a detailed discussion of Freud's position and also discusses how other forms of sexual desire have been pathologised:

De Block, A. and Adriaens, P.R. (2013) 'Pathologising sexual deviance: A history', *Journal of Sex Research*, 50(3–4): 276–98.

Disability

Wendell, S. (1996) *The Rejected Body: Feminist Philosophical Reflections on Disability*. London: Routledge.

Age

Rader, F. (1979) 'The social construction of ages and the ideology of stages', *The Journal of Sociology & Social Welfare*, 6(5): Article 6.

Class

Criab, I. (2002) 'What is social class?', *Group Analysis*, 35(3): 342–50.

Poverty

This is an American text, but increasingly relevant to Britain:

Smith, L. (2010) *Psychology, Poverty and the End of Social Exclusion: Putting Our Practice to Work*. New York: Teachers College Press.

4
Reclaiming Identity in the 1970s and 1980s

'This is who we are!'

Learning aims

- To understand how grassroot political movements of the 1970s and 1980s enabled some of those stigmatised by 'race', gender, sexuality, disability and class to develop positive identities. Although radical at the time, many ideas that the political movements of this period popularised have become widely accepted and so understanding them is important even when working with othered clients who do not seem to be particularly politically engaged.
- To develop some familiarity with the marginalised identity development models inspired by these movements.
- To use the information, questions, exercises and other resources in this chapter to consider whether, and how, these identity development models might inform your practice.
- To consider how your own identity statuses impact your therapeutic work.
- To think about how you and your client's marginalised identity status work with or against each other.

Perhaps the most insidious and soul-destroying effects of living with hostility are those that impact how we see ourselves. There are several ways of thinking about how identity is impacted by our social context. A psychosocial perspective, such as Charles Horton Cooley's (1902) concept of the 'looking-glass self' suggests that identity is informed by our impressions of how other people perceive us. A psychodynamic perspective might suggest that to be othered is to become a receptacle for the mainstream's unwanted psychic material.

However one thinks about being othered, constructing a positive identity is clearly a psychological necessity. The construction of positive marginalised identities began in grassroot political movements of the 1950s, 1960s, 1970s and 1980s. This chapter discusses the marginalised identity development models that were inspired by these movements and which remain relevant to many clients (and therapists). You may find it useful to read this chapter from your marginalised as well as from your mainstream positions.

The Marxist notion of 'false consciousness' is helpful in understanding marginalised identity development models. False consciousness refers to a way of thinking that prevents the working class from being aware that they are being exploited. William Edward Burghardt Du Bois's (1903) 'double consciousness', which involves always looking at one's self through the eyes of white people and judging oneself by their standards, is also a helpful concept, and can be extended to think about other mainstream/marginalised pairings that have an abusive social relationship.

Both these ideas feed into the more recent idea of internalised oppression. Internalised oppression involves identifying with the interests of your oppressor and unquestioningly accepting values that serve only their interests. It also involves accepting a degrading narrative about your own group and a flattering narrative about your oppressor. Marginalised identity development models track a process of moving from internalised oppression to pride in one's identity and a commitment to social justice. They differ from other kinds of identity development theories in that they trace social rather than individual identity development.

Becoming black

Du Bois saw the development of pride in one's race as an important step in personal liberation. As black consciousness developed in America from the Civil Rights era onwards, developing a positive and proud black identity became seen as important for psychological reasons as well as political reasons.

Theories of black identity development, greatly influenced by Du Bois (1903) and by the Civil Rights Movement, were introduced by African American academics from the 1970s onwards. These models trace the process by which African Americans stop identifying with mainstream white culture and develop a positive identification with African and African American culture. William Cross (1971), who developed one of the most influential racial identity models, calls this the 'Negro-to-Black conversion'.

The original racial identity models described a linear, stage-by-stage developmental process, but were later revised to describe complex, non-linear states rather than stages. Janet Helms (1984) introduced the concept of 'ego statuses' rather than developmental stages, each status having its own constellation of attitudes, emotions, beliefs, motives and behaviour. Tudor and Naughton (2006) elaborate the difference between Helms's use of 'ego status' and the way the term is used in Transactional Analysis). All Helms's statuses may be present in a client's – or therapist's – psyche, with one predominating at any given time, or the predominant status may be a blend of other statuses.

Cross and Helms later adapted their models to apply to other visible racial and ethnic groups. The following is a (much abbreviated) amalgamation of several racial and ethnic identity models, modified from Robert Carter (1995).

- Pre-awareness–Unexamined identity

    'Nobody's ever treated me unfairly'

This status may manifest as denial or acceptance of the status quo. It is characterised by low self-esteem, compliance, subservience, idealisation of mainstream culture, and repressed rage and blame (Vandiver, 2001).

- Encounter–Dissonance

    'That hurt! The only way to protect myself from prejudice is to stick to my own people (but actually I'm more familiar with mainstream society so I feel an internal dissonance, as if I do not really belong anywhere)'

A client or therapist usually moves into this stage as a result of being subjected to racial or ethnic hostility, or as the result of a strongly positive interaction with members of their own group. This stage/status is characterised by acute or chronic anxiety, confusion about who one is and feeling as if one does not belong anywhere. There may be an idealisation of the marginalised community, and guilt and anger in relation to one's previous acceptance of status quo.

- Immersion–Emersion

    'My own community is totally awesome, unlike the horrible racist community that I'm rejecting' (immersion)

    'My own community has its faults like any other, and the community that I'd rejected has its good points too' (emersion)

This stage/status is characterised by a process of immersion in one's marginalised community, followed by an emergence back out into the larger community from a rooted and more confident place. Those in the immersion–emersion stage generally feel good about their race or ethnicity, and feel angry with the mainstream community.

- Internalisation–Commitment

    'I feel comfortable in my own skin wherever I am' (internalisation)

    'I am active in trying to bring about greater social justice' (commitment)

Those in this status/stage have internalised the positives of immersion and have a sustainable commitment to social justice. This stage/status is characterised by confidence in one's racial or ethnic identity, ideological flexibility and psychological openness. In an early model (Thomas, 1971) the final stage manifests as the person being relatively free of personal conflicts regarding gender, class and age as well as race and ethnicity.

It is, however, important to remember that the models are American, and may not work elsewhere. One client that I worked with used the term 'black' when referring to herself, but was clearly not comfortable doing so:

> 'You looked really uncomfortable when you said the word "black" there. I imagine it has very different connotations in Zimbabwe than it does here'.
>
> 'Yeah, it has colonial overtones because colour is only relevant in the context of colonialism. Otherwise you're Shona or Ndebele or whatever'.
>
> 'So do you think of yourself as Shona rather than as Zimbabwean?'
>
> 'Both'.
>
> 'Depends on the context?'
>
> 'Of course'.

Case study

Charity, an older black woman from a country that was a part of the British Empire, adores the Queen and the Royal Family. She arrived in great distress for a session with her therapist, Michael, after a colleague had made a racist remark about Meghan Markle, who was, at the time, the Duchess of Sussex. Charity had been very hurt indeed by the remark and as Michael listened, he could hear that her hurt went back decades. The hostility and social abuse that had greeted Charity when she arrived to work in the new NHS had been an enormous shock to her, but she had never lost her intense pride at living in Britain.

Over the next few sessions, the pride that she had always taken in the Queen and the Commonwealth gave way as she spoke about the misery of living in an environment that had always been hostile towards her, and in which she had never felt valued or respected. The soul-destroying hurt that she had felt pressing in her chest for most of her life transformed into anger. Michael, having done the personal work necessary, was able to listen to and contain Charity's anger. However, although he was not shaken by her fury, she was. The transition from Acceptance to Encounter–Dissonance shakes something foundational as one understands the painful reality of one's standing in the social world. Michael understood this and was careful not to rush Charity through this destabilising transition.

Cross's and Helms's models are about changes in political consciousness that might occur, and reoccur, at any stage of life. Jean Phinney's (1990) model, on the other hand, looks at the development of ethnic identity in childhood and adolescence. Phinney is concerned with psychological function rather than political involvement.

Cross (2016) argues that Phinney's concern with whether or not someone feels good about their marginalised-group membership (and therefore has higher self-esteem) changed the focus of marginalised identity models from the well-being of the community (through political and social action) to the well-being of the individual. In a revision of his Negro-to-Black model, Cross acknowledges that not identifying with a marginalised group that you belong to does not necessarily mean that you reject that aspect of your identity – those for whom their membership of a marginalised group is simply not very significant simply construct their identity around another feature of their lives, and are as likely to be as psychologically healthy as someone who has gone through the linear stages of the early models and is politically active. It makes no difference, psychologically, what your self-esteem is based upon, but it does make a difference politically.

> **Self-awareness exercise**
>
> If you are a racially or ethnically marginalised therapist, think, write or talk about whether, and how, the above statuses manifest in your understanding of yourself. If you are mixed race, your turn will come in the next chapter. If you are white your turn comes in Chapter 10.

Racial-identity development models are tools that can be used to better understand your client, yourself and your relationship, but may not be a good fit for everyone. Cross (1991) actually revised his thinking on racial identity and racial-identity models quite substantially in his later career. He moved his focus away from the internalised racism that bids black people identify with their oppressor and onto the resilience and 'adaptive fortitude' that preserves psychological well-being in the face of hostility.

Becoming a woman (who will not be kept down)

Feminism, as it was understood in the 1970s and 1980s, may be out of favour with some contemporary political activists, but it did usher in new ways of being women – and men – that are now taken for granted. Nancy Dowling and Kristin Roush's 1985 feminist identity development model is based on William Cross's Negro-to-Black identity development model, and might be summarised as:

Passive acceptance: I'm fine with what is expected of women

Revelation: I'm angry about what is expected of women, and I'm angry with a system that enables unequal treatment and with those who exploit it

Embeddedness–emanation: I feel more comfortable with women than men, and most comfortable with other feminists

Synthesis: Not all men are bad

Active commitment: I am active in trying to bring about greater social justice

Feminism has become mainstream since Dowling and Roush's model was researched and developed, as evidenced by the #Me Too, #Time's Up, #Enough's Enough and #Say Her Name campaigns and the Women's Marches. A recent use of a feminist identity scale that is based on Dowling and Roush's model (Kucharska, 2018) finds that women are, these days, unlikely to completely withdraw from men when in embeddedness–emanation.

However, embeddedness–emanation is also about making a positive connection with other women, and finding strength in that connection. The client in the case study below was not able to do this.

Case study

Dawn was becoming more than a little tired of the 'banter' that she had no choice but to listen to at work. She had initially found it funny and was flattered to often be the centre of attention. She began to feel uncomfortable at work after a friend was sexually assaulted while on holiday. Her manager noticed that she was no longer up for a giggle, and, thinking that she must be depressed, referred her to the company's employee assistance programme.

Chris, the therapist she saw, also thought that Dawn was depressed, and this was borne out by her CORE scores. When asked, Dawn realised that she did indeed feel tense most of the time, and isolated. Her enthusiasm had indeed dwindled. She did find herself avoiding talking with colleagues. She did feel like crying a lot of the time. Chris explained the different types of negative thinking and asked Dawn to keep a record of recurrent thoughts.

When they were looking at how these thoughts affected Dawn's mood, Chris noticed that Dawn generalised about men a lot. When she tried to challenge this way of thinking, Dawn became increasingly disengaged. Chris remarked on this and Dawn asked if she could talk about something that had happened. Chris sat back and just listened as Dawn spoke about her friend's assault and then about the atmosphere at work. Chris recognised this atmosphere – where sexual violence against women was normalised and excused – as rape culture.

When listening to Dawn talk about her friend's assault, Chris had been listening out for an irrational fear of being assaulted herself, but instead heard about a catalogue of micro-assaults from colleagues. None of them involved touch, but they were assaults on Dawn's dignity and personhood. Rather than understanding Dawn's mounting unease at work as resulting from irrational ways of thinking, Chris now understood it to arise from working in a hostile atmosphere. The work that followed in their remaining session focused on what Dawn might do to change the culture in her workplace.

Dawn resigned from work two weeks after her sessions ended. Had Chris known about feminist identity models, she might have realised that she was expecting Dawn to jump from Revelation to Active Commitment. Dawn was virtually the only woman in her workplace and had found herself battling alone. Had Chris approached the therapy from a social justice perspective, she might have given herself permission to become an advocate and to intervene at an organisational level so that the workplace culture could be addressed systemically.

> **Reflective exercise**
>
> Depending on whether you are working alone or with others, and whatever your gender identification, think, write or talk about where you would place yourself in relation to Dowling and Roush's model.

Becoming glad to be gay

Identity was central to the Gay Liberation Movement of the 1970s and 1980s. Unlike 'race', sexual orientation is not visible, and so 'coming out' was understood as a form of political activism with gay men and lesbians refusing to stay invisible. The early gay identity development models were very much influenced by this emphasis on coming out.

> **Fun fact**
>
> The phrase 'coming out' originates with the huge drag (cross-dressing) balls held in New York and other American cities in the early twentieth century that parodied debutante balls. 'Coming out' in this context did not refer to coming out of hiding, but to joining a community of peers. Its more recent meaning of coming out of hiding (coming out of the closet/wardrobe that one jumped into to avoid being discovered in bed with a same-sex partner) began in the 1960s, but the idea of coming out as a means of combating social shame and changing public prejudice dates back to 1869.

Like early racial identity models, early gay identity models tended to assume that identity is developed stage-by-stage, although some propose processes rather than stages. These models, some of which are listed below, may be summarised as:

Identity confusion: what am I?

Identity comparison: I am different

Identity tolerance: I am probably gay

Identity acceptance: I am gay

Identity pride: I am glad to be gay. I'm glad my friends are gay too because the straight world is oppressive and I am committed to changing it

Identity synthesis: I happen to be gay – and I am also many other things too

Vivienne Cass's 1979 model, which was based on research with gay men, and validated in 1984 with a lesbian research population, provided the basis of many of the later models and remains widely used (Cass, 1979, 1984). Suzanne Degges-White, Barbara Rice and Jane Myers revisited Cass's model in 2000 (Degges-White et al., 2000) and questioned whether Cass's pride stage was as relevant today as it was in the 1970s and 1980s.

Cass's pride stage, like the immersion stage in racial identity models, and Dowling and Roush's feminist emersion–emanation stage, is adversarial – the overall process can be understood in Transactional Analysis(ish) terms – beginning, in relation to the mainstream, with 'You're ok; I'm not ok', moving to 'I'm ok; you're not ok' before arriving at 'I'm ok; you're ok (although you have some issues you need to deal with)'. Only some of the lesbians that Degges-White et al. (2000) interviewed had held an 'us and them' attitude, and only for a short while. Few had ever seen their identity as lesbians as the main aspect of their identity.

Richard Troiden had already suggested in 1989 that coming out should be seen as an option rather than evidence of self-acceptance (Troiden, 1989). Susan McCarn and Ruth Fassinger (1996) make a distinction between accepting that you are gay and seeing yourself as part of the gay community. They too see coming out as an option rather than a progression towards a mature identity, and as always happening in a particular context (coming out in Uganda, for instance, is a very different matter to coming out in San Francisco).

Movements such as the Civil Rights Movement, Black Power, Feminism and the Gay Liberation Movement changed social attitudes. Kucharska (2018) and White, Rice and Myers (2000) are not the only commentators to suggest that adversarial aspects of models forged in the heat of politically charged times might be out-dated. However, many of the gains made by these movements are slipping away as draconian policies are enacted on those seen as 'other'; time will tell how this impacts the relevance of the adversarial stages of these models.

> **Case study**
>
> Jay, now in her 60s, was very active in the Gay Liberation Movement of the 1970s and 1980s. She moved abroad in 1990 to pursue her career, then returned to live in England. Appalled by the rise in hate crime following the Brexit referendum (Townsend, 2016; Travis, 2016), she decided to become politically active again.
>
> However, when she sought out other politically active gay people, she found herself in a largely unfamiliar world. Her therapist, Huiyin, was 25 and identified as Queer (see Chapter 5 for a definition of Queer). Huiyin understood that Jay felt alienated partly because she did not understand the philosophical thinking behind gender non-conformity. She was aware of an urge to educate her, but managed to stay focused on Jay's emotional experience. Jay, who had been initially doubtful about working with a therapist who was so much younger, felt that Huiyin really 'got' her.
>
> Huiyin did not know it at the time but she had laid the foundations for working so well with Jay when, wondering if she might be a lesbian, she had read a lot of gay fiction. She had an imaginative appreciation of the Gay Liberation Movement in the 1970s and 1980s and understood that as well as feeling alienated from the community she wanted to be a part of, Jay was coming to terms with the loss of the community that she *had* been a part of.

> **Reflective exercise**
>
> If you identify with any of the stages in the above model reflect on what it is like for you to be there. If you are at any of the later three stages, think back to how you felt in the earlier three. In what ways do you think the journey might be similar and different for gay clients of a different generation?

Nothing about us without us

Chapter 2 presented disability as something that results from social exclusion rather than from physical impairment. This is known as the 'social model' (or sometimes the 'minority model') of disability and is contrasted with the 'medical model' that constructs disability as a medical problem to be solved. The construction of disability as a medical problem has, in the past, led to disabled people living in huge institutions where they could be easily 'treated', rather than in their own homes. The slogan 'nothing about us without us' is used by disability rights activists to demand that no policy should be decided upon without full participation of those it affects. The social model is about affirming disability as a social creation and a political issue.

The social model has been the basis from which the Disability Rights Movement has campaigned against social exclusion. The Disability Rights Movement in the UK places a particular emphasis on disability as resulting from oppression. In the USA, the preferred term is 'people with disabilities', which puts the person first. In the UK, the preferred term is 'disabled people' because people are disabled by the social environment – if the social environment were not excluding, disabled people would not be people with disabilities, they'd just be people.

There are a number of different kinds of disability identity development models. Jennifer Gibson's (2006) model might be summarised as:

Passive Awareness: 'I'm no different to anyone else' (childhood)

Realisation: 'Why me?' or 'It won't stop me' (adolescence)

Acceptance: 'I am happy to be disabled – that is who I am. I value the company of other people with disabilities, and I am comfortable in the wider social world too' (adulthood)

Case study

Tom had been referred to me by his GP and was not happy about it. He was distant, glaring. It took a while to establish that he would rather stay for the session than leave, and a while longer to explore whether, regardless of the GP's diagnosis of depression, there was anything *he* thought it might be useful to talk to me about.

Tom had been born without legs, and had, as far as he could remember, always felt fine about this – it was who he was and always had been. He said that everything had changed when he got a pressure sore. He hated his body, he hated his life and he hated himself.

There was something about Tom and his fury that was deeply familiar. As I tuned in to what this might be, I became very aware that I was sitting opposite a 15-year-old. I became able to hear how the pressure sore had collided with adolescence in a way that had made both unbearable. The constant – and painful – medical procedures necessitated by the pressure sore were a deep affront to his emerging need for separation and privacy. His dignity was wounded in a way that it had not been when he was younger.

He hated his parents, as many people experiencing adolescence do, and he hated that he was more dependent upon them than his friends were upon theirs. He was angry and tearful when talking about his friends whom he knew wanted to go to a particular club that was not wheelchair accessible, but hadn't – or so he believed until he heard that a group of them had gone and not mentioned it to him.

And he did not mention the pressure sore to his friends. He did not want to. But he did want to talk to somebody. He could see that his parents couldn't handle it (and, he added quietly, that he knew they were frightened by his anger). He'd hoped the GP might understand, but he'd just looked awkward when Tom told him that he hated being disabled, and referred him to some stranger (me).

> Tom and I were able to work together over a long period, during which the pressure sore healed. He negotiated a new identity as a young adult and also moved into the Acceptance stage of Gibson's model. He re-evaluated many of his friendships, not solely on the basis of feeling excluded but also on the basis of how he wanted to spend his time. He didn't actually enjoy clubbing very much, but was interested in sport.
>
> He began to play wheelchair basketball – and everything changed again. He was able to be gentler with his parents once he had a physical outlet for the energy and aggression of adolescence. And he met his 'tribe' – other young men with whom he felt a connection. He stopped seeing many of his other friends for a while, but they reconnected at the funeral of a mutual friend who was stabbed in a random attack. Tom was much more at ease within himself by the time they reconnected, and was able to connect with them in a way that honoured their (nearly) life-long friendships but also made space for him to be confident in himself as well as confident in them.

> **Reflective exercise**
>
> Whether you identify as disabled or not, and depending on whether you are working alone or with others, think, write or talk about what the word 'disability' means to you.

Class acts

The modern labour movement has a longer history than some of the movements discussed above, and Marx's analysis of class enabled generations to develop proud and empowered working-class identities yet, until recently, there has been no psychologically based model of class identity development. This reflects a more general lack of interest in class and therapy. The number of books and articles published on therapy and class has been a mere trickle, compared to the deluge of publications on race, culture, gender, sexuality and (to a lesser degree) disability. However, this seems to be changing. William Liu's prolific work on counselling and class is written from an American perspective but it can also be helpful to therapists in Britain and elsewhere. Joanna Ryan (2017) has recently published a book on class and psychoanalysis and Anne Kearney's 1996 *Counselling, Class and Politics* was reissued in 2018 (Kearney, 2018).

Recent class identity development models come from Nicholas Ladany and Maryann Krikorian (2013) and from William Liu (2011a, 2011b, 2013). Ladany and Krikorian present their model as 'phases of means of interpersonal functioning of people from financially challenged social classes' rather than as an identity development model, but the overall process has striking similarities to the development models already discussed in this chapter. These can be summarised as:

Adaptation: 'You get what you work for'

Incongruence: 'That wasn't fair ... or at least I don't think it was'

Exploration: 'It wasn't at all fair, and the whole class system is not at all fair'

Integration: 'The whole system is unfair in relation to lots of other issues too. This really saddens me, but I think things can change'

William Liu's Social Class and Classism Consciousness Model (2011b) also focuses on a client's sense of being in an unjust social system. It has three broad levels – no social class consciousness, social class self-consciousness and social class consciousness – and ten statuses within each level. Liu (2011a) has also developed a Social Class Worldview Model which offers an understanding of the beliefs, attitudes and values that we use to understand and interpret class. Rather than focusing on the development of political activism, the premise of this model is that we use a combination of human, social and cultural capital to be on a par with others in our social class – 'keeping up with the Joneses' – and that we experience stress when we cannot do so. Unfortunately there is not space to do Liu's models justice here but they are worth exploring further.

Case study

Harry was a self-made man who, despite growing up in poverty, had built his own business from scratch. He often expressed contempt for those amongst whom he had grown up when speaking to his therapist, Amber. Amber inwardly winced a little every time he did so, but knew that his contempt was entangled with anger and humiliation that arose from having been physically and emotionally abused as a child. She understood his contempt as one of the ways in which Harry tried to distance himself from his childhood and so she worked with his feelings about his family rather than directly challenging the contempt he expressed for people who might well have been amongst her other clients.

After working with Amber for a few weeks, Harry, by chance, bumped into Jake, with whom he had been friends as a child. Jake had insisted that Harry come to a family barbecue that he was having that weekend. Harry had lived with Jake's family for short periods when he had to escape his father's alcoholic wrath as a child, and had been envious of the secure and loving atmosphere in Jake's home.

Harry was subdued when he saw Amber the following week. He had not intended to stay long at the barbecue. As he had guessed, Jake lived in a run-down housing estate, and although it was not the estate in which they had grown up, Harry nevertheless found being there depressing and was worried about leaving his BMW parked in Jake's street. However, the warmth with which he had been greeted by Jake's extended family had taken him by surprise. He became tearful as he talked to Amber about Jake's parents. Seeing them again had brought back memories of feeling cared for when he'd stayed with them as a child. It became evident to Amber, and later to Harry, that they had actually played a significant part in enabling Harry to survive his childhood.

Harry went to visit Jake's parents a couple of weeks later and found them looking after Jake's children while he was at work. They told Harry that Jake had given up work to look after his wife while she was dying of motor neuron disease. He had been left as the sole parent to their three children, and had previously worked delivering mail because he could fit his hours around taking the children to school. He had recently been laid off and now worked uncertain hours as a carer. Although as jovial as ever, Jake's parents looked very tired. The children were a handful to say the least.

The following weekend Harry went to see Jake with a takeaway for the whole family and a few beers for later on. Once the children were in bed, they drank the beer and talked into the evening. When Harry had his next session with Amber, she remarked on how indignant he sounded when he mentioned that Jake could only claim financial support for two of his children. Harry looked confused, and then talked about how he had, when it was introduced, approved of the policy of capping child benefit at two children, but that he did not think it fair that Jake was struggling even though he was working. Being with Jake's family had clearly unsettled him – and moved him from Adaptation into Incongruence in the above class identity model.

Over the next while, Harry began seeing Jake and his children quite often. He talked to Amber about the affection he felt for them and his mounting outrage at seeing then gradually slip into poverty despite Jake working very long hours when there was work to be had. When Harry declared that he was going to give Jake quite a large sum of money, Amber suggested that they explore this. Harry was able to acknowledge a desire to be seen as a generous benefactor, and once he and Amber had worked with this, he was able to acknowledge that acting in this way would likely wound Jake's pride and damage rather than deepen their friendship.

Once Harry was able to see past his need to be admired, he found that he was developing genuine respect for Jake who carried on being a good father, a loving son and a compassionate carer despite being constantly exhausted and worried about money. He genuinely wanted to help. However, he was also beginning to see that the stresses in Jake's life were largely caused by many of the welfare reforms and austerity measures that Harry had approved of when they were introduced, and that whatever financial help he could give Jake would only ease things temporarily. This insight moved him from Incongruence into Exploration.

With Amber's encouragement, Harry continued to help Jake out in ways that did not call attention to themselves. Going to Jake's on a Friday evening with a takeaway and some beer became a routine, and since they were drinking, he stayed overnight. If Jake was working the next day, Harry took the kids out, not to somewhere flashy and expensive as he'd initially planned, but to a climbing wall in another part of the city. Harry liked that the kids were challenged by learning to climb – he still believed in determination and overcoming obstacles, and in any case, climbing burned off the kids' excess energy. They were much calmer after a Saturday morning at the wall, which was a relief to Jake who was worn out after a morning racing around hoisting people out of bed and making sure that he gave out the right medication.

(Continued)

He observed to Harry one Friday night, while watching the football, that the kids were doing better at school and that one of the teachers thought that this was because learning to climb had taught the kids how to focus. Harry had never thought of the ability to focus as being something that needed to be developed. His own steely determination had been a defence against the pain of his childhood and had, as far as he could remember, always been there. He too had noticed that the kids were less chaotic. He smiled. He felt that he had done something really worthwhile. Harry knew that Jake was thanking him in his characteristically understated way and felt no need for any more from him. He did share his pride with Amber though and revelled in the sense that something he had done had made a real difference.

This sense of satisfaction helped Harry move from Exploration to Integration. He had grown increasingly uncomfortable with the views that he had held when first working with Amber, and the derogatory language that he had used to express them. He started paying more attention to politics and thinking in a more critical way. He changed the news outlets that he used and began to see the impact of austerity and welfare reform on all kinds of people that he had previously been dismissive and scornful of. He also negotiated a deal between the management of the climbing wall and the school Jake's children went to and climbing became part of the school's physical education curriculum.

Self-awareness exercise

Depending on whether you are working alone or with others, think, write or talk about how you identify in class terms and how you feel about your identification.

Practising with care

Marginalised identity development models do several very useful things. They remind us that:

- Changes in the social and political environment impact how we see ourselves and other people, and, conversely, changes in how we see ourselves impact the social and political environment
- There may be a difference between how we – or a client – are identified and how we ourselves identify
- Not all members of a marginalised group relate to their group in the same way
- The way in which someone relates to their marginalised identity may change, often dramatically, over their lifespan
- Feelings about one's marginalised identity – and about the mainstream community – will vary depending upon the status one is currently inhabiting.

Perhaps the most important thing that marginalised identity development models bring is the idea that the identity status of both the marginalised client *and the marginalised therapist* impact the therapeutic relationship (mainstream identity statuses also impact the therapeutic relationship, and will be discussed in Chapter 10).

Denial and acceptance

A marginalised client who feels ashamed of their 'difference', or who is relatively unaware of being seen as different, may be disinclined to seek out a therapist from their own marginalised group (though they may well be given such a therapist).

A marginalised therapist in this status may feel anxious about working with a client who is marginalised in the same way that they are.

Angst and ambivalence

A client who feels ambivalent about their marginalised status is likely to be slow in engaging therapeutically with a therapist from their own group, or even overtly rejecting. Dionne Joseph (1995) breaks a taboo in writing about being racially abused by black as well as white clients.

Marginalised therapists in this status may feel uncomfortable at the prospect of working with a client who is marginalised in the same way that they are, and may have concerns about being 'black enough' (or the equivalent).

More politically correct than thou

A client who is immersed in identifying strongly with their marginalised group may only be open to working with a similarly marginalised identity if the therapist meets their standard of political awareness. Robert Carter (1995) suggests that black therapists working with a black client in Immersion should be prepared for a 'blackness' test. He also warns that such a client may understand the therapist's educational and professional accomplishments as collusion in a world that the client is rejecting.

Therapists in this status are likely to want to educate their same-group clients about their shared cultural heritage or shared political interests. Depending on where the client is in terms of identity development, this may be ill-timed.

Being comfortable with yourself and other people

A client in this status understands that although they will get different things from a marginalised and a mainstream therapist, both might be of value. They are likely to attach at least as much significance to the practitioner's therapeutic qualities as they do to their social position.

A therapist in this status is generally at ease working with someone from their own marginalised group and usually understanding of their client's identity development process.

Therapeutic relationships can be matched – as when the therapist and client are in the same status – or mismatched. There are many possible pairings, each throwing up particular challenges. Should both client and therapist be in denial-acceptance, there is a danger of the therapist using their professional status to nurture (and possibly express) a feeling of superiority in relation to a client from the same marginalised group, especially if there is a difference in status between them within the group as well. Both may feel anxious about seeing the other. A therapeutic relationship in which both are ambivalent about their own identity would be off to a difficult start, and the therapist would need to work very hard to prevent their own material leaking into their relationship with the client. A therapist and client who are both immersed in identifying strongly with their marginalised group may work very well together, or may find it difficult to stay focused. If both client and therapist are comfortable with their marginalised identity they are likely to work well with each other and to be able to make background use of some shared social experience. In unmatched therapeutic relationships, it is (obviously) preferable for the therapist to be in a more developed status.

Conclusion

Although potentially very useful in helping us understand 'where a client is at', marginalised identity models should be used with care because:

- They are based on generalised research results and cannot adequately capture the complexities of real people, or variation in life experience
- Identity development models may be useful with some clients and less useful with others
- These models were developed and validated in particular contexts, e.g. the USA, mostly in the 1970s, and with sample populations that will inevitably have had their own particularities. They may not be so relevant in a different context.

How you use marginalised identity development models – or not – will very much depend upon your therapeutic approach and your understanding of the therapeutic relationship. Several studies have shown that those who have a strongly positive identification with their marginalised identity are more resilient to the psychological wounding discussed in Chapter 1. For this reason, some therapists introduce identity development as a therapeutic task and use identity development models in an educative way. Others use them only to understand, and do not actively try to move the client's process along.

Whatever your way of working, marginalised identity development models are useful in reminding us that it matters where we are in relation to where the client is. It is not difficult to see that a therapist who is experiencing confusion and ambivalence in relation to their own marginalised identity is going to struggle to gain the respect and trust of a client who is not. A therapist in an immersion status may experience frustration with a client who identifies more readily with the mainstream. The potential variations are numerous, and each needs to be thought about in context. Supervision is a good place to do this.

Further reading

On racial identity

The actor David Harewood, on breaking down psychologically when caught in a web of conflicting demands with regard to how black people are seen and see themselves:

Harewood, D. (2017) 'I feel no shame about my mental breakdown: It helped make me who I am', *The Guardian,* 13 October. Available at: www.theguardian.com/commentisfree/2017/oct/13/mental-health-sectioned-black-identity (accessed 19 September 2017).

Helms, J.E. (1986) 'Expanding racial identity theory to cover counseling process', *Journal of Counseling Psychology*, 33(1): 62–4.

Phinney J. (1990) 'Ethnic identity in adolescents and adults: Review of research', *Psychological Bulletin*, 108: 499–514.

On being gay, and coming out

Adams, T.E. (2010) 'Paradoxes of sexuality, gay identity, and the closet', *Symbolic Interaction*, 33(2): 234–56.

Ali, S. and Barden, S. (2015) 'Considering the cycle of coming out: Sexual minority identity development', *The Professional Counselor*, 5(4): 501–15.

Disability

Summarises different disability identity models:

Forber-Pratt, A.J., Lyew, D.A., Mueller, C. and Samples, L.B. (2017) 'Disability identity development: A systematic review of the literature', *Rehabilitation Psychology*, American Psychological Association, 62(2): 198–207.

Class

This is not a recent publication, but remains a very valuable resource:

Hill, M. and Rothblum, E.D. (eds) (1996) *Classism and Feminist Therapy: Counting Costs.* Binghamton: Harrington Park Press.

Hudson, K. (2019) *Lowborn: Growing Up, Getting Away and Returning to Britain's Poorest Towns.* London: Chatto & Windus.

Liu, W.M. (ed.) (2013) *The Oxford Handbook of Social Class in Counseling.* New York: Oxford University Press.

A novel about class mobility and working-class friendships:

Smith, Z. (2016) *Swing Time.* London: Penguin.

Surridge, P. (2007) 'Class belonging: A quantitative exploration of identity and consciousness', *The British Journal of Sociology*, 58(2): 207–26.

5
Contemporary Identities

'And we're here too!'

Learning aims

- To be better equipped to work respectfully, particularly with younger clients, by understanding how contemporary thought has changed the way in which many understand their identity in relation to 'race', sexuality, gender and disability.
- To understand how those who have been made invisible by binary categories are asserting their presence and constructing positive identities, and so be better equipped to work respectfully with mixed-race, gender non-conforming and intersex identities.
- To consider how class identities are also changing, and so be able to work with greater awareness and sensitivity.

The liberation movements that the previous chapter referred to were based on binary differences: black/white, women/men, gay/straight, disabled/able-bodied. A newer politics has been emerging over the last couple of decades that challenges this either/or-ness by undermining concepts such as 'race' and gender (and so you may find it useful to review Chapter 2 before, or as, you read this chapter). Much of this new way of thinking has been useful to those who remained painfully unseen and unheard in the 1970s and 1980s. The 1990s ushered in the new politics, spearheaded by those who do not identify with the binary either/or-ness that underpins so many social categories. It is important to have some awareness of these newer ways of thinking as they profoundly impact how many clients – particularly younger clients – understand their social identities.

Drawing your own box

In writing about her biracial identity Meghan Markle (2015) recounts being asked to choose one parent over another by a form demanding that she tick a box declaring whether she was white, black, Hispanic or Asian. When a teacher told her just to tick white, she had an acute understanding of how deeply this would hurt her mother (who would put on a brave face). Her father, whom she could see was quietly furious when she recounted what had happened, told her that if she was ever asked to choose a 'race' again she should draw her own box.

The British government has allowed people to identify as being of more than one 'race' from the 1991 census onwards (2000 in the USA), largely as a result of campaigning by activists. There is a new 'race' politics emerging that seeks to expose the whole idea of 'race', and therefore of racial purity, as the hoax that it is. In time we will, perhaps, surpass the need for boxes – and for racial identity development models.

However, it seems that, for now, racial identity models are still potentially useful, and a new generation of theorists has developed biracial identity development models. These models look at how those who have parents of different 'races' resolve the very particular issues that they face.

The very early models make grim reading. Everett Stonequist (1961), one of the earliest theorists in biracial identity, saw biracial people as condemned to a life of what he calls an 'identity purgatory', fitting in neither here nor there, perpetually in the margins of society. Like other racial identity models, Stonequist's model was developed in the USA, and so reflects particularities of the USA's racial history, specifically the anti-miscegenation laws that banned interracial marriage (and in some states, interracial sex). In the glare of such intense hostility towards interracial relationships, it is perhaps understandable that Stonequist was pessimistic about the prospect of forming a positive biracial identity. More recent models are more optimistic, but still present being biracial as inherently difficult, and in doing so perhaps speak most strongly to those countries with a history of anti-miscegenation laws.

Carlos Poston's (1990) Biracial Identity Development Model revolves around the demand, which potentially comes from family as well as from society, that a child choose one potential racial identity over another. As Markle's article shows, this amounts to effectively asking a child to choose one parent (and their side of the extended family) over another. Making such a choice leads to feelings of distance from the not-chosen parent, guilt and self-hatred. If these feelings are resolved then, according to Poston, the child moves to the next stage, incorporating elements of the denied identity, before finally integrating both identities. If the feelings of distance, guilt and self-hatred are not resolved, the child does not move on.

Although based upon earlier black racial identity development models that address the impact of racism, Poston's model, bizarrely, does not. Maria Root (1990), who takes a sociological perspective, does acknowledge the impact of racism. She also suggests that early identity struggles in relation to race, family, acceptance, difference and isolation reoccur at different points in later life. She suggests four potentially positive resolutions:

- accepting the identity society assigns to you
- identifying with only one racial group
- identifying with both (or all) racial groups
- identifying with other multiracial people.

A client (or therapist) potentially chooses different resolutions at different points in their lives. Poston's model is developmental – there are stages to move through (or not) and a final ideal outcome. Root does not see any of her resolutions as more mature than another. Nor does she see them as mutually exclusive – somebody might identify in more than one way at the same time, or move among a number of identities. Building on Root's work, Kristen Renn (2008) found that some of the students who participated in her research refused to identify themselves in terms of 'race', thus resisting the whole notion of 'race'.

Some use the term 'dual heritage' rather than 'mixed race'. I will use the term 'mixed race' as I want to keep an emphasis on (the social reality of) 'race' and racism. Someone with a Swedish mother and a white South African father has a dual heritage, but they will not be asked to choose one racial identity over another, and they will not have their racial identity questioned. I also use the term 'mixed race' rather than 'biracial' so as to include those whose ancestry is of multiple rather than of two 'races'.

The experience of being mixed race is very much dependent upon the context, i.e. where and when, and biracial identity models should be used with the client's specific context(s) very much in mind. Although the proportion of mixed-race people is higher in Britain than in the USA, numbers are increasing rapidly on both sides of the Atlantic. Demographers predict that, in time, most people will be mixed race. Clearly, racial identity development models will need to develop or cease – in order to keep up with changing social contexts. Meanwhile, it is important to remember that not everyone who has parents of different 'races' identifies as mixed race – the British rapper Akala (2018) says that he always identified as black, rather than as mixed race because he knew that other people (such as the police) would see him as black.

Case study

Alex had grown up with his white mother, who had sent him to an exclusive private school and he talked a lot in his first few sessions with James about how this had prepared him for the fiercely competitive atmosphere of high-level

(Continued)

> finance. James initially assumed that Alex, who was brown, and seemed thoroughly immersed in an affluent, white world, was at the early stage of racial identity development models such as those discussed in the previous chapter. James was a little thrown on discovering that Alex also had a close relationship with his father's extended family, and that he clearly also identified as Jamaican. His supervisor suggested that he might find biracial identity development models helpful in understanding how someone can 'be both'.

From Gay Lib to LGBTQQIAAP+

Mixed-race people were sometimes viewed with suspicion in Black politics (the lighter skinned were seen as suffering less racism), and so too were bisexual people viewed with suspicion within the Gay Liberation Movement (on the grounds that they could revert to a mainstream heterosexual identity when it suited them). Although bisexual people are now, in theory at least, under the LGB (lesbian-gay-bisexual) banner, many still feel marginalised.

Barbara Gormley (2018) suggests that bisexuality is potentially threatening to those who identify as gay as well as those who identify as straight because it challenges the homosexual/heterosexual binary that underlies their identity. One of the undermining forces identified by the Gay Liberation Movement was heternormativity, or the presentation of heterosexuality as the norm, as what is 'natural'. The contemporary Bisexual Movement is concerned with mononormativity (you're either gay or straight) as well as heteronormativity – and homonormativity.

There are a number of bisexual identity development models based on the gay identity models discussed in the previous chapter. However, perhaps the most significant finding comes from Klein and colleagues' (1985) relatively early research. They found that sexuality often changes over time, and so conceptualised sexuality as a process. In finding this, and in considering 'heterosexual', 'homosexual' and 'bisexual' to be inadequate and simplistic classifications, they pre-empt more contemporary ideas about sexual orientation being fluid (changing over time). The research shows that this is not the case for everybody, but much (though not all) of the research suggests that women's sexuality tends to be more fluid – as perhaps demonstrated by the recent same-sex marriages of numerous high-profile women (including Susie Orbach) who were previously in long (and happy) opposite-sex marriages. Increasing numbers of people are drawing their own box when it comes to sexuality as well as racial identification.

Other boxes that have been drawn in recent years include 'asexual' (sometimes referred to as 'ace'), 'questioning', 'pansexual', polysexual and skoliosexual.

Asexuality

Asexuality is different to celibacy. Those who choose to be celibate have decided not to act on sexual attraction. Those who are asexual do not feel sexual attraction in the first place (except 'grey' asexuals – as in 'grey area'– who do experience sexual attraction very occasionally, only slightly, or only in specific circumstances and 'demisexuals' who experience sexual attraction after they have formed an emotional bond – not necessarily a romantic bond – with someone). Some asexual people experience romantic (not sexual) attraction and have romantic relationships. Others do not. Sexless romantic relationships can be hard to find and so there are websites that help those who want love without pressure to have sex (for example, www.asexualcupid.com/uk/). Some asexual people are attracted to another person's appearance, but without romantic or sexual feelings (this is called 'aesthetic attraction'). Others experience sensual attraction, or the desire to have sensual, affectionate, non-sexual contact.

Some people who are asexual masturbate; others do not. The important distinction between sexual and asexual people with regard to masturbation is that someone who is asexual would not want to be sexual with another person, even if they fantasise about that particular person. Many asexual people do have sex with other people. Sometimes (but not always) this is because they feel pressurised to do so. Such pressure will not necessarily come from another individual, but from social expectations that everyone should have a satisfying sex life (and some asexuals do, just not with a partner). Therapists have a particular propensity towards seeing an absence of sexual desire as a problem, an attitude that is unhelpful to those already feeling under pressure to have unwanted sex.

Pansexuality, polysexuality, skoliosexuality and questioning

Pansexuality, or omnisexuality, has come into greater public awareness of late as celebrities including Miley Cyrus and Kristen Stewart have come out. Pansexuality differs from bisexuality as an identity in that there is an emphasis on being open to all sexes and genders including intersex, transgender, agender, multigendered, fluidgender and gender-queer partners. It differs from polysexuality in that polysexuals are not attracted to all gender variations. Skoliosexual people are attracted to gender non-conforming people. 'Questioning' is adopted as a sexual identity by those who want to create a pressure-free space in which to explore their sexuality and/or gender identification. Some use terms such as 'bi-curious', 'gay-curious' or 'heteroflexible' instead.

Thinking about oneself as pansexual – or as bisexual, heterosexual, skoliosexual or asexual, etc. – is a matter of identity rather than sexual behaviour. Many people, for example, have same-sex encounters, but do not identify as gay or bisexual, and the same is true of many gay people who have opposite sex encounters. Nor is sexual identity also necessarily related to sexual experiences. Pansexual people identify as being potentially interested in anyone, regardless of their gender identity. It does not necessarily mean that they have, or have had, sex with people of all gender identities.

Gender non-conforming

The way that many people think about gender – and sex – is also changing. Chapter 2 discussed the distinction between gender roles and biological sex.

That chapter also briefly introduced Judith Butler's work on gender. Butler's (1990) argument is that as gender is an enactment of an abstract idea, 'doing gender' in non-conforming ways – 'gender trouble' – is a subversive act that challenges the institution of gender. Enacting the gender associated with the opposite sex, as the drag artists that Butler studied for her PhD research do, is an example of gender non-conformity. Butler (1993) reduces the distinction between sex and gender by arguing that one's biological sex never comes without expectations of how to be a man or a woman – i.e. gender – and so the two are never really separate.

Butler has been steadfast and vocal in supporting the rights of everyone to do gender in whatever way they choose and her ideas about gender have been influential within the gender-nonconforming community. It may therefore be useful to have at least a broad understanding of her arguments when working with a client who sees themselves as a gender rebel. However, it is also important to be aware that some activists have a strong antipathy towards Butler's ideas and view gender as something that one knows one truly is.

Increasing numbers of people – particularly young people – are choosing to identify in gender non-conforming ways, such as:

Agender or gender neutral: someone who does not identify with a gender

Aliagender or third gender: someone whose gender identity is other than masculine or feminine

Androgyne: someone who identifies as both masculine and feminine

Bigender: someone who identifies with two distinct genders, such as femininity and androgyny

Boi: a person of colour who identifies as being masculine, but not as being a man

Butch: most often used by 'masculine' lesbians, but also by masculine queer men and queer people of other genders ('queer' is discussed below)

Demiboy: someone who identifies partly as a boy and partly as another gender

Demigirl: someone who identifies partly as a girl and partly as another gender

Female to male or FTM: a transgender or transsexual person who was assigned female at birth but has transitioned to male

Feminine-of-centre: someone who feels, and often presents, as feminine but may not identify as a woman

Feminine presenting: someone who expresses gender in a feminine way

Gender creative: someone who does not enact gender stereotypes, but does not necessarily identify as transgender

Gender fluid: someone whose gender identity and presentation fluctuates between masculine, feminine, both and neither

Genderless: someone who does not identify with any gender

Gender non-conforming: someone whose gender expression does not conform to mainstream notions of masculinity and femininity

Gender questioning: someone who is questioning their current gender identity and exploring others

Gender variant: someone whose gender identity does not conform to the sex that they were assigned at birth

Intergender: someone whose gender identity falls between genders

Male to female or MTF: someone who was identified as male at birth but has transitioned to female

Masculine-of-centre: someone who feels, and often presents, as masculine but may not identify as a man

Masculine presenting: someone who expresses gender in a masculine way

Mx: used instead of Mr or Ms for someone who identifies as neither a man nor a woman

Neutrois: an umbrella term for people who do not identify as either a man or a woman. Agender, non-binary and genderless people may also identify in this way

Non-binary or enby or NB: someone whose gender identity is other than male and female

Pangender: someone who experiences all gender identities either simultaneously or over time

Polygender: someone who experiences more than one gender identity either simultaneously or moving among genders

Third gender: this term has a variety of meanings depending on who is using it. It can mean someone who is intersex or someone who does not identify as a man or a woman

Trans: sometimes used as shorthand for transsexual or transgender (see below) and sometimes to include a wider range of identities

Trans*: an umbrella term that refers to all of the identities within the gender identity spectrum, other than cisgender man and cisgender woman. Trans (without the asterisk) can be intentionally used to describe trans men and trans women, while the asterisk denotes a special effort to also include all non-binary, genderqueer, and gender non-conforming identities, including (but not limited to, and in no particular order) transgender, transman, transwoman, transsexual, genderqueer, genderfluid, non-binary, genderfucked, genderless, agender, non-gendered, third gender, two-spirit and bigender

Transfeminine: someone who was assigned male at birth, identifies and presents as feminine but may not identify as a woman or a transgender woman

Transgender: an inclusive term for people whose gender identity and/or gender expression differs from the sex they were assigned at birth. Some transgender people take hormones and some have surgery, but a transgender identity is not dependent on either

Transman: someone who was identified as female at birth, but has transitioned to male

Transmasculine: someone who was assigned female at birth, identifies and presents as masculine but may not identify as a man or a transgender man

Transsexual: someone who has transformed their body with medical intervention. This term is associated with medical and psychological discourse and now out-dated.

Transwoman: someone who was identified as male at birth, but has transitioned to female

Trigender: someone who identifies with three genders

Queer: used to be a pejorative term for gay people, who then reclaimed it and used it with pride. It is now more often used as an inclusive term for all those who are, in whatever way, sexually and/or gender non-conformist. The deconstruction of constructs such as gender or heteronormativity is fundamental to academic Queer Theory and is a way of understanding the social world that is commonly understood by activists and young people in general.

The following terms are also useful to understand when working with gender non-conforming clients:

Ally: someone who is (usually) cisgendered and heterosexual, but who actively supports queer rights

Cisgender: someone whose gender corresponds to the sex they were assigned at birth.

It is important to remember that there is a difference between gender identity and gender expression. Someone may, for instance, identify as non-binary but present as feminine – or masculine. Gender identity is increasingly understood to be an individual matter, and it is, perhaps, for this reason that there has not been a proliferation of identity development models, although Aaron Devor (2004), himself a transman, does present a model. He emphasises that as each person is unique the model cannot possibly apply to everyone in the same way and that he intends it only to provide insights into a commonly, but not universally, followed path.

Case study

Belle had recently transitioned from male to female when she started seeing Carl for therapy. She began saying that she was nervous about being in therapy again because her previous experience of therapy had not been good. Carl wanted to ask for some more detail about this, but Belle had already begun crying – and seemed to have moved on. Carl kept quiet and listened. Belle seemed to be saying that she was not happy because she still looked 'like a man'.

However, as Carl listened more carefully, he realised that what Belle was complaining about was the way that people looked at her. His careful enquiries revealed that she felt exposed and very negatively judged. He wanted to know how she felt about her appearance, but had a sense that now was not the time to ask. They stayed with Belle's distress at being judged. She brought up her relationship with her father in a torrent of tears.

Belle described how her father had mocked her appearance in front of her family and neighbours (she kept her friends far, far away from him). Over the next few weeks of work, it became evident that Belle's father had belittled her since she was a child and that his horrifically cruel taunts about her still looking like 'a f***ing bloke' were in keeping with the way he habitually spoke to her. This became the focus of the therapy – much to Belle's relief. Much of the literature on working with Trans* clients emphasises the risk of the therapist becoming transfixed upon their client's gender identity to the exclusion of other issues. Belle's previous therapist had focused upon Belle's appearance. Belle had left in frustration when she'd given her one tip too many about how to appear more feminine.

Belle was actually pretty happy with her appearance – not completely happy, but, as she said with a coy smile, what woman is? Her distress did not result from her transition, but from her relationship with her father and the self-consciousness that arose from a lifetime of being belittled and mocked. Therapy helped Belle to recognise and nurture a sense of peace within herself that had arisen since she had transitioned. This helped her to be more robust in the face of hostility from her father and from strangers.

Intersex

Intersex activists – and many doctors – are demanding that future generations of intersex children are not subjected to 'treatment' before they are old enough to decide if this is what they want. A number of countries have already changed the medical guidelines and, in some cases, the law.

Ending surgery on babies has been the focus of political activism. Some intersex people would also like to draw their own box. Three sexes are now legally recognised in several countries, although Britain is yet to issue an intersex birth certificate. Others are happy with the gender identities assigned to them at birth, i.e. they identify as male or female rather than intersex. The birth of the intersex community and its subsequent political tensions are discussed in Hida Viloria's biography, which is recommended in *Further Reading* at the end of this chapter.

> **Case study**
>
> Marguerite, who was now 17, had a complicated childhood abroad after her parents died in a car accident, and had been mainly brought up by her grandfather. She had been seeing Viki, her therapist, for seven months before telling her that she thought that there was something wrong with her genitalia. Although Viki was aware that many people worry unnecessarily about this, she was neither reassuring nor dismissive. Encouraged, Marguerite told her that although she did not remember hurting herself or having any surgery, she could see scarring. She was clearly very fearful.
>
> Viki decided against suggesting that she ask her GP to examine her, and instead referred her to Wendy, a psychosexual doctor whom she knew worked with great sensitivity. Marguerite saw the doctor several times before she felt comfortable enough to be examined. Wendy confirmed Marguerite's suspicion that she had had surgery. It proved impossible to find Marguerite's early medical records, and so she and Wendy worked together to make sense of what had happened to her physically and what this would mean for her future.

L stands for lesbian
G stands for gay
B stands for bisexual
T stands for transgender
Q stands for queer
Q stands for questioning
I stands for intersex
A stands for asexual
A stands for allies
P stands for pansexual
+ stands for all other gender and sexuality identities

You don't look disabled to me

The 'disabled' box may also be subject to change. A handful of researchers in disability studies are suggesting that the social model excludes many disabled people and so needs to be tweaked if not replaced altogether in order for the movement to become more inclusive. Tom Shakespeare (2002) argues that the social model can be summed up by the slogan, 'disabled by society not by our bodies', and that its success, both in fostering positive identities and winning legal rights, is due to its simplicity. Its problem, he argues, is that it is also simplistic.

Shakespeare suggests that although it has become politically taboo to say so, people are also disabled by their impairments. Impairment and disability should, he suggests, be described as different places on a continuum. Some people who use wheelchairs because they have illnesses such as myalgic encephalomyelitis (ME) or fibromyalgia are disabled by the environment when out and about, but disabled by their symptoms when too exhausted to get out of bed. Shakespeare's position is widely seen as being dangerously close to the medical model, which is seen by most activists as being in opposition to a civil rights approach, and so his work is hugely controversial.

Mairian Corker (1998) is also concerned with the social model's emphasis on physical barriers excluding those already excluded from mainstream society by communication barriers. Corker is not advocating that the social model be abandoned but rather that it is used in an inclusive way. Understanding disability as arising from both the built environment (inaccessible buildings, etc.) and the social environment (signers not being available, conditions that are distressing to those on the autistic spectrum, etc.) extends the model to make it more inclusive.

Awareness of hidden disabilities is increasing. Hidden disabilities are those that are not evident to other people. Clients tell me that one of the difficulties of having an illness such as ME, fibromyalgia and multiple sclerosis is that others seem to find it hard to understand that they can be relatively well one day, but very unwell the next. Many clients have neurological differences that were not recognised in childhood. Several books, including Mark Haddon's *The Curious Incident of the Dog in the Night-time* and Luke Jackson's *Freaks, Geeks and Asperger Syndrome* have brought the mild end of the autistic spectrum to public awareness, but many clients grew up in a time in which the only people who had ever heard of it were speech therapists. I have worked with several clients who were really struggling – and I was really struggling to understand – until we considered the possibility that they were on the autistic spectrum. Similarly, other neurological differences such as dyslexia, dyscalculia and dyspraxia are often not apparent to others, sometimes because they show up in ways that they do not recognise.

Case study

Although Una's client, Mahinder, is emotionally intelligent and seems keen to work in therapy, she is habitually late for sessions. Una has encouraged Mahinder to explore what this is about several times but has not been able to get past superficialities about losing car keys or just running late. When Mahinder arrives fifteen minutes after the session was due to begin, claiming that she got lost on the way, Una becomes insistent that they explore what is going on. She points out that Mahinder has been driving to her consulting room for six months, and that it really isn't possible that she got lost. Mahinder is very resistant to exploring what Una has assumed is a fear of what therapy will uncover, but eventually concurs with this understanding. Six weeks later, she again arrived very late, again claiming to have got lost, this time with a story about road works. Una did recall a slight diversion but could not imagine how this could possibly have caused Mahinder to take the bizarre journey that she described.

(Continued)

Una was, in her life outside therapy, trying to find appropriate support for her dyslexic nephew. A couple of evenings after her session with Mahinder, she was researching online when she came across a chat room of dyslexics commiserating with each other about becoming hopelessly and shamingly lost. It stopped her in her tracks. As far as Una knew, Mahinder had no problems with reading and writing and could tie her own shoelaces. She read more of the posts. They did sound very like Mahinder.

Una moved on to another website and gradually realised that most of what she thought she knew about dyslexia was wrong. After reflection, supervision and several weeks of listening in a more sensitised way, she told Mahinder that she thought of her several times while looking at a website about the strengths as well as the problems associated with dyslexia, and wondered if Mahinder might want to take a look to see if she recognised herself. Mahinder did have a look – and recognised herself very quickly. She was initially wary of seeking an assessment and diagnosis as she feared discrimination at work, but eventually decided to do so. She used the test results, which confirmed that she was indeed dyslexic, to find ways of working with her difficulties and also working with the strengths that being dyslexic had brought her.

Self-awareness exercise

The distinction is sometimes made not between disabled and able-bodied, but between disabled and not-disabled-yet. Depending on whether you are working alone or with others, think, write or talk about your response to the likelihood that you will, at some point in your life, become disabled (or, if you already identify as disabled, think, write or talk about the likelihood that, as you grow older, you acquire another impairment).

Changing class identities

There are also changes in the way that people understand their class identity – or not. The contemporary class researchers, Mike Savage and his colleagues (2013) on The Great British Class Survey, whose work was introduced in Chapter 2, found that although their participants were aware of class as a political concern when, for instance, voting, many did not self-identify in terms of class. When asked if they ever thought of themselves as belonging to a particular class, 19 per cent of Savage's 2003 survey respondents said they were middle class, 26 per cent said they were working class and 53 per cent said they did not belong to a social class.

Savage suggests that the low percentage of those identifying as middle class might be a reflection of middle-class lifestyles being presented as the norm (working-class lifestyles, on the other hand tend to be sensationalised, as they are on reality television, for example). Those who enact norms see themselves as normal, and so, as Savage and colleagues (2005) suggest, middle-class people see themselves as 'just normal'. The percentage of people who identified as working class was not as low as those who identified as middle class, but it is still low. Beverley Skeggs's (1997) hypothesis that working-class women are particularly resistant to identifying as working class has already been discussed in Chapters 1 and 2. She suggests that while there are still some positive images of traditional working-class men in our social imagery, the same cannot be said for working-class women, who feel thoroughly ridiculed. It also may be the case that people become more aware of class when in transition. Elizabeth Aries and Maynard Seider (2007) found, for instance, that working-class students in elite private schools were more aware of their social-class position than students in state education.

Both Joanna Ryan (2017) and Anne Kearney (2018) emphasise the importance of working therapeutically with class-inflicted wounds – particularly shame – and encourage the therapist to broach the subject of class even if this makes the client uncomfortable. However, assuming that Savage's reclassification of class (discussed in Chapter 3) is useful, and that categories such as 'new affluent workers' and 'precariat' do provide a better model of contemporary socio-economic hierarchies, it seems reasonable to assume that some clients may simply not know how to identify in terms of class.

A client whom The Great British Class Survey would identify as a new affluent worker is unlikely to come from a middle-class background, unlikely to share the cultural tastes of the traditional middle class, yet be very well paid. I am seeing two such clients at the moment, and the way in which they think of themselves in terms of class is very different. One takes a lot of care in presenting as middle class, and social acquaintances are surprised if she tells them that she grew up in poverty. She feels a little fraudulent most of the time. My other client moved to a middle-class area, but does not feel at home there and has not made friends. She feels more comfortable in her partner's flat in a traditional working-class area.

Class is in a period of transition. Meanwhile, socio-economic inequality is increasing. It is, perhaps, more important to work with the wounds inflicted by economic injustice than it is to insist on talking about class per se.

Case study

Jade takes pride in how she, as a single mother, is bringing up her son, Kyle. She started feeling low when the 'bedroom tax', which reduced the amount of benefits she was entitled to because she had a spare room in her old flat, had forced her to move away from her family. The company that had employed her as a carer offered her work nearer her new home but her mother was now too far away to look after Kyle while Jade was at work and, as the work was irregular, putting Kyle in a nursery was not a cost-effective option. She was not able to

(Continued)

accept the offer of work. Nor was she able to claim benefits for a number of weeks as she was considered to be voluntarily unemployed. Her savings had dwindled when she'd had to replace her fridge and then her washing machine. She'd used the rest while waiting for her first Universal Credit payment. Once receiving Universal Credit she'd been sanctioned for being late for an appointment because Kyle had a lying-on-the-pavement-screaming tantrum on the way there. She no longer had enough money.

Jade had been on antidepressants since her move, but had no sense that they were still helping. A new GP referred her to a local counselling agency. Jade was initially very reluctant to talk, but eventually told Craig, who was assessing her, that she'd been referred to a food-bank, but had not yet managed to make herself go. Kyle had been fed, but she had not eaten for two days. She had been brought up in a household that 'wasn't fancy, but we never went hungry'. Her parents had always taken pride in providing enough, plus the odd treat. Jade saw the food-bank as proof that she had failed as a parent. She had not had enough money to visit her parents for some time and had made excuses to stop them from visiting her because she did not want them to see how bare her cupboards were.

Craig's heart sank. Although his agency had been a free service in the past, it had been forced by cuts to its funding to insist on a donation of at least £5. It was abundantly clear that Jade could not afford this, and that she was likely to leave feeling even more humiliated than she'd felt asking for psychological help in the first place.

He told Jade that the agency would be in touch with her once a suitable therapist became available. He raised the issue of the minimum donation discriminating against the poorest clients with the agency, and after a very intense debate managed to negotiate an agreement whereby a generous private donation that had recently been made by an ex-client could be used to fund clients who really could not afford to pay anything. When he offered this option to Jade, she again felt searing humiliation at being offered more charity but after initially refusing, she realised that what she could really not afford was for her mental health to deteriorate any further, and reluctantly accepted.

Her therapist understood the shame that Jade felt at not providing, at 'not coping', the humiliation she endured when interacting with the Department of Work and Pensions (DWP) and the humiliation that comes with the dehumanising effects of poverty. She knew how important it was that she work with all of this – and that she do so with delicacy. Jade eventually arrived at a place in which she realised that she was doing all she could to help Kyle feel secure despite all the unwelcome changes in their lives – and to realise how much her little boy missed his granny. She swallowed what was left of her pride and invited her mother to visit.

Her mother's behaviour was a little out of character from the beginning of her visit. She stayed in the living room while Jade made her a cup of tea and put the biscuits she'd brought on a plate. She made it very clear that she was delighted to see Jade, but did not ask how she was doing. Instead she hinted that she and Jade's father were rather lonely (this was not true) and told Kyle how much she missed looking after him (which was true).

Jade's mother also took great pride in how she looked after her children. She had been aware of the problems people were having whilst moving from the old benefits system to Universal Credit and had worked out that if Jade was having the same problems they would be the straw that broke her back financially. She and her husband, who received a navy pension as well as a state pension, were in a position to help Jade financially, but knew that if they were to do so, Jade would either have to declare what they gave her to the DWP and have it be counted as income, thereby losing some of her Universal Credit or, if she kept quiet about it, be guilty of benefit fraud.

After the most delicate dance around the subject, Jade's mother said that she and Jade's father were thinking of moving to a bungalow so that they would not have to cope with stairs as they got older, and asked her if this bungalow happened to be bigger than their current house, she would think about whether she and Kyle might, at some point in the future, think about living with them. Both she and Jade knew that this was an invitation to come home now. Jade and her parents were able to move to a bigger house (though not a bungalow) close to where Jade had grown up and she found herself back in the bosom of the traditional working-class community she had grown up in. This return had been facilitated not only by her mother's tact, but also by her therapist's ability to work sensitively with shame.

Reflective exercise

Pick several clients and think about how they may have been wounded by their class background. Are you already working with these wounds? If not, how might you do so?

Intersectionality

One of the most important recent theoretical developments that is of immediate relevance to therapists trying to understand how socio-political forces impact a client is intersectionality. Like many of the other black theorists mentioned in this book, Kimberlé Crenshaw, who introduced the notion of intersectionality, is not always given credit for what has become a hugely influential theory; nor Patricia Hill Collins for developing it.

Crenshaw (1998) uses the metaphor of an intersection to illustrate how black women are simultaneously hit by racist traffic coming from one direction and sexist traffic from another. Collins extended Crenshaw's theory to those at the intersections of different forms of discrimination. Nobody has one single social identity. Everyone, whether a client or therapist, is seen, and in some way sees themselves, in terms of 'race', class, age, ethnicity, sex/gender, sexuality, dis/ability and religion (including no religion). Some of these identities give us social, political and economic advantages, and some disadvantage us and expose us to hostility. Many people are exposed to disadvantage and hostility from multiple routes and so might be said to live on a roundabout of disadvantage and hostility.

Being a legal scholar, Crenshaw suggests that the ambulance that comes to help those hit by discriminatory traffic represents the law, but the ambulance can also represent you the therapist. If you are solely concerned with, say, racist or homophobic traffic, you will not see the traffic coming from other directions. As therapists, we need to see the bigger picture.

Crenshaw's theory of intersectionality illustrates a 'more than the sum of its parts' principle. Her point is not that black women have racism to deal with in addition to sexism (though, clearly, they do) but that they are impacted by both simultaneously – and invisibly. Crenshaw argues that we think about 'race' and gender separately, and that because we think about black men when we think about 'race', and about white women when we think about gender, black women become invisible. One of the legal cases that she discusses was brought by a group of black women who complained that General Motors was discriminating against them. The company had a history of not employing black women. This had changed, but all the black women it did employ subsequently lost their jobs during a layoff and they did not employ any more. The court examined the case through the lenses of both racial and sexual discrimination and found that as the company employed black men in the plant, and white women in the office, it was guilty of neither sexual nor racial discrimination.

Intersectionality has become a much used and sometimes over-diluted theory. When used to merely acknowledge that each of us belongs to a number of social groups, the theory rather loses its point, and those who live in the intersections of systems of exclusion become invisible – again. Crenshaw's theory was intended to help the courts think about the experience of life at intersections. It can help us do the same.

Case study

Much of the research into the particular kind of cancer that eventually killed Simone used data from an almost all-white population. Simone did not know that, as someone whose forebears were from a particular part of Africa, she was at a much higher risk, and neither did her doctor. She accessed therapy through a community service for people with cancer. Her presenting problem was not her impending death, but how she was going to manage in the interim.

She and her husband had been foster parents and she had been a full-time foster mother to Jason after her husband had become frustrated by her pre-diagnosis lethargy and left. Jason, now 18, had just moved out of her home when she was diagnosed. Knowing that it would be unethical for her to begin another foster relationship when she was so depleted and might soon experience disturbing symptoms, she talked about plans to look for other work. It quickly became evident that she did not have the energy for even a few hours of light work.

She applied for Universal Credit and was dismayed when she was assessed as being fit for work. Her therapist, Emil, knew that if Simone challenged the assessment it was very likely to be overturned and so prioritised finding an agency that would support her through this process.

But he did not do so at the expense of working with Simone's increasing despair about her immediate future. She had never known her maternal grandparents, who had disowned their daughter when she had married an African man in the late 1960s. All connection with her father's family had been lost after he died in an industrial accident when she was a baby. Her mother had been in long-term psychiatric care since her husband's death. Simone had no other family that she knew of and had spent most of her childhood in care.

She was very frightened of becoming isolated as she became less well. She spoke to her therapist, Emil, about the possibility of asking Jason to move back in with her, and her ambivalence about doing so. Jason had been late for a Universal Credit Work Search Review because he had a panic attack on his way there and had paused to regain his composure. He had been sanctioned and was no longer coping financially. Simone wondered if it would make more sense for them to pool their resources. She was also worried about his safety as a particularly vulnerable young black man. She worried about police harassment. She worried about knife crime. She worried about gangs.

Emil referred Simone to a support group for other women living with cancer. More white women than black get cancer and the makeup of the group certainly reflected this. Simone noticed several of the group members look taken aback when she appeared. There was a subtle change in the atmosphere. The facilitator greeted her a little too brightly. Simone felt self-consciously black and found herself feeling uneasy whenever she was persuaded to speak. When reflecting on the experience of being in the group with Emil a few days later she said only that she hadn't felt comfortable speaking in the group.

It was at this point that her therapeutic relationship with Emil began to unravel. It did not occur to him that there might be a racialised element to Simone's experience in the group and she was not sure he would understand if she tried to explain why she thought there had been. Emil knew that, as Simone was, for now, relatively well, he could not offer her many more sessions and he had become a little over-invested in her finding the group useful. She felt increasingly pressured and misunderstood as he tried to work with her anxiety about speaking in public and her 'difficulty in accepting support'.

Simone needed Emil to understand what it was like to be dying because you are invisible to researchers. To slide into poverty because you are invisible to politicians. To be assessed as fit for work when one is dying. She needed him to understand what it is like when the man you love and thought would take care of you fails to see that you are ill and walks out because you've 'let yourself go'. She needed Emil to understand how invisible she felt as a mother to children that were not her own. And, most of all, she needed him to understand what it is like to be invisible while sticking out like a sore thumb, to understand how painful it is to be looked at without ever being seen.

There was an air of mutual exasperation when they ended.

Conclusion

Dos and don'ts

Do remember that we all have several social identities. Understanding a client (or yourself) in terms of only one social identity – gender or class, for instance – is inevitably misleading.

Do remember that the significance a client's social identities have for them may change in response to social and political conditions. Being disabled, for instance, has, for many people, a new significance in times of governmental austerity.

Do remember that any or all of someone's social identities may differ over time. Someone may identify as straight during one part of their lives, for instance, and as Queer during another.

Do remember that any or all of someone's social identities may be different in different contexts. Someone who is mixed race may be considered – and consider themselves – white in one context and black in another.

Do remember that the significance (or 'salience') of a particular social identity may change over time. Being gay, for instance, may take up a bigger part of life at 18 than it does at 80 – or not. A particular identity may become more or less significant as a result of a change in the person or their circumstances.

Do remember that the meaning that someone attaches to an identity may differ from its significance to others. A client may be relieved to identify as asexual, while this is a worry to those around them – perhaps including their therapist.

Do remember that different aspects of a client's identity may be salient in different contexts. A client's gender identity might be foregrounded while they talk about their social life, but class may be more salient when they talk about work.

Do remember that clients use the ideas about identity that are culturally available to them. Older clients may *tend* to use the ideas discussed in the previous chapter, while younger clients may *tend* to use the ideas discussed in this chapter.

Do remember that some social identities are at an intersection of different systems of marginalisation, and that the impact of living at an intersection is more than the sum of its parts.

Do remember that most people, possibly yourself included, are both advantaged and disadvantaged by their various social identities.

Do find out, either by asking or careful listening, what identity terms (and pronouns) your client prefers.

Do consider being open about identifications that you hold that are not apparent. Whether or not this would be appropriate with a particular client will probably depend on the context and should therefore be discussed in supervision.

Don't assume a client's racial identification on the basis of how they look.

Don't assume a client's sexual identity on the basis of their current partner's gender.

Don't assume a client's gender identification on the basis of how they look and dress.

Don't assume whether a client is disabled or not.

Don't assume a client's class identity on the basis of their accent.

Don't assume a client's religion on the basis of how they dress.

Don't assume that a client's 'difference' is the issue that they want to work with in therapy.

Further reading

Race

Miville, M.L., Constantine, M.G., Baysden, M.F. and So-Lloyd, G. (2005) 'Chameleon changes: An exploration of racial identity themes of multiracial people', *Journal of Counseling Psychology*, 52(4): 507–16.
Nadal, K.L., Wong, Y., Griffin, K., Sriken, J., Vargas, V., Wideman, M. and Kolawole, A. (2011) 'Microaggressions and the multiracial experience', *International Journal of Humanities and Social Science*, 1(7): 36–44.

A novel that explores the complex ways in which biracial children are impacted by the race (and gender) wounds of their parents:

Ng, C. (2014) *Everything I Never Told You*. London: Penguin.

Gender

Barker, M. (2017) *Gender, Sexual, and Relationship Diversity*. Lutterworth: BACP.
Lenning, E. (2009) 'Moving beyond the binary: Exploring the dimensions of gender presentation and orientation', *International Journal of Social Inquiry*, 2: 39–54.
Lester, C.N. (2017) *Trans Like Me*. London: Virago.

Sexuality

A novel that brings an older Caribbean man and his partner to the contemporary Queer scene:

Evaristo, B. (2013) *Mr. Loverman*. London: Penguin.
Galupo, M.P., Ramirez, J.L. and Pulice-Farrow, L. (2017) '"Regardless of their gender": Descriptions of sexual identity among bisexual, pansexual, and queer identified individuals', *Journal of Bisexuality*, 17(1): 108–24.
Scherrer, K.S. (2008) 'Coming to an asexual identity: Negotiating identity, negotiating desire', *Sexualities*, 11(5): 621–41.
Weinberg, M.S., Williams, C.J. and Pryor, D.W. (1994) *Dual Attraction: Understanding Bisexuality*. New York: Oxford University Press.

Intersex

An autobiographical account of living as an intersex person who did not have medical intervention as a child:

Viloria, H. (2017) *Born Both: An Intersex Life*. New York: Hachette Books.

Disability

Gabel, S. and Peters, S. (2004) 'Presage of a paradigm shift? Beyond the social model of disability toward resistance theories of disability', *Disability & Society*, 19(6): 585–600.
Taylor, R. (2005) 'Can the social model explain all of disability experience?: Perspectives of persons with chronic fatigue syndrome', *The American Journal of Occupational Therapy*, 59(5): 497–506.

Class

Hudson, K. (2019) *Lowborn: Growing Up, Getting Away and Returning to Britain's Poorest Towns*. London: Chatto and Windus.
Rollock, N., Vincent, C., Gillborn, D. and Ball, S. (2012) '"Middle class by profession": Class status and identification amongst the Black middle classes', *Ethnicities*, 13(3): 253–75.

Both of these novels look at the impact on class identities of the 1980s banking crisis – Lanchester's set in London, and Craig's in a rural setting:

Lanchester, J. (2012) *Capital*. London: Faber and Faber.
Craig, A. (2017) *The Lie of the Land*. London: Little, Brown.

Intersectionality

Crenshaw, K. (1989) 'Demarginalizing the intersection of race and sex: A black feminist critique of antidiscrimination doctrine, feminist theory and antiracist politics', *University of Chicago Legal Forum*, 1, Article 8: 139–67. Available at: http://chicagounbound.uchicago.edu/uclf/vol1989/iss1/8.
Crenshaw, K. (1991) 'Mapping the margins: Intersectionality, identity politics, and violence against women of color', *Stanford Law Review*, 43(6): 1241–99.

SECTION II

BRIDGES AND BARRIERS TO THERAPEUTIC WORK

'CAN WE MEET?'

6
Cultural Arrogance

'Shall we meet at my place?'

Learning aims

- To thoughtfully consider the dangers of enculturation and cultural imperialism within the therapeutic relationship.
- To be aware of the dangers of simplified knowledge.
- To think critically about the culture-specific guidelines in the cross-cultural counselling literature.

Many of the social groups discussed in the previous chapters may be thought of as having their own culture – gay culture, queer culture, black culture, working-class culture, youth culture, deaf culture and so on. The mental health professions have a history of offering bad or inadequate services to clients from these groups. As discussed earlier, theorists have attempted to remedy this by identifying three main areas of training and professional development. The preceding chapters focused upon developing an understanding of social power structures. Chapters 9 and 10 look at how to develop an awareness of one's own biases, prejudices and privileges. This chapter and the next focus on developing cultural understanding and developing the ability to work in culturally appropriate ways.

Focusing on culture sometimes elicits the 'saris, samosas and steel bands' criticism, i.e. that it ignores issues of power and inequality, and that systemic racism cannot be mended by 'cultural appreciation'. Indeed it cannot, but the cultural aspects of working with the marginalised 'other' are also important – and also involve thinking about power and inequality. This chapter discusses the dangers of enculturation – a mind-set in which you see your own cultural norms and values as 'right', and do not understand or appreciate other cultures.

Much of the literature consists of information about other cultures that is intended to help therapists work in culturally appropriate ways. Unfortunately, this can give the impression that culturally competent practice is merely a matter of learning some facts about other cultures and adapting your practice appropriately. This chapter argues that although cultural understanding is very necessary, it is also much more elusive than this literature sometimes suggests – and vulnerable to misuse.

Welcome to 'our' world

There is a danger that in trying to help the 'other', 'we' practise a kind of cultural imperialism by subtly imposing our own worldview or understanding of what is real, what is important, what is right and what is 'healthy'. Therapy's tendency to see itself as scientific can fool us into thinking that it will be universally helpful. What we (whoever we are and wherever we come from) find helpful is to some degree dependent upon what we think the problem is. A client from another country or ethnic community may understand their distress very differently to the way that you understand it.

In some communities, distress may be understood not as something that originates within an individual, but rather as a disturbance in family or community relationships or as a disturbance in the relationship between the community and the natural world and/or the spirit world. Distress may be understood as resulting from malign magic, for instance, or spirit possession, or an imbalance in internal qualities such as warmth and dampness. Remedies and preventative measures may include community meetings, sacrifice, offerings, prayer, wearing amulets, massage, acupuncture, herbal treatments or a change of diet.

There is an interesting debate as to the appropriateness of exporting therapeutic methods that originate in the global north in response to humanitarian crises in the global south. Andrew Solomon (2008) describes how a survivor of the Rwandan genocide told him that his community had to put a stop to 'help' from Western mental health workers who wanted survivors to sit, one by one, in dingy rooms, talking about the horrors they had endured, rather than being out in the sun, drumming to get their blood flowing again and being uplifted by the support of their community. This book is not concerned with the appropriateness of therapy as part of an international aid package, but the debate is of relevance as some clients who have fled from war or persecution in other countries are referred for therapy quite quickly after arriving in Britain.

One such client, Prossy Kakoozan (Kakoozan in conversation with Boyles, 2017), who worked with several therapists, recounts what was and was not helpful. She emphasises the importance of making sure that clients understand what therapy entails and how it might help. She also identifies as helpful:

- a proper explanation of the different kinds of therapy available
- being able to choose what kind of therapy to have
- the therapist understanding something about the client's country and how help is given there
- the therapist being knowledgeable about the client's social and political context, but not using this background knowledge to make assumptions about the client's feelings
- therapist personalising rather than generalising client's problems
- being treated as a person rather than a client
- feeling a connection with the therapist

and as unhelpful:

- feeling pressured into therapy
- therapy being time-limited
- intrusive questions
- cultural and political ignorance
- ignorance of the asylum system
- finding a therapist condescending
- therapist seeming distracted
- therapist leaving the room to consult a supervisor
- therapist focusing on the childhood origins of trauma
- premature referral to group therapy.

> **Reflective exercise**
>
> Depending on whether you are working alone or with others think, write or talk about the story your therapeutic approach tells about:
>
> - what causes psychological disturbance
> - what relieves psychological disturbance
>
> The foreign 'other' is not alone in being unfamiliar with what therapy is and how it works. Although ideas from therapy – the unconscious, positive thinking, it being good to talk, etc. – have been widely adopted into popular culture, many indigenous clients may not understand how therapy, or a particular kind of therapy, works.
>
> Depending on whether you are working alone or with others, think, write or talk about how you would explain what therapy is and how it works to Yves, a forced migrant from Rwanda, and how you would explain it to Peter, a stiff-upper-lipped 80-year-old from the Home Counties. Would you explain it differently, and if so, why?

But it would be a mistake to assume that a client from another country will necessarily be unfamiliar with therapy. Therapy is enjoying an international boom.

There are an estimated 400,000 trained therapists in China where there is something of a 'fever' for counselling (Branigan, 2014). There is a counselling service in every school in Taiwan, and in many schools in India, where therapists now make up a significant proportion of helping professionals. Private practitioners in India and Pakistan have no shortage of clients (BACP, 2013).

Therapy is international, but this does not mean that a client from another country will be any more familiar with the inner workings of therapy than a client from your own country might be. The many different therapeutic approaches can be understood as comprising distinct cultures in themselves, each with its specialised language, its own particular ways of understanding the world and particular expectations as to how one should behave. We are, generally, not very good at recognising how mysterious – and excluding – these cultural practices can be to any client not already 'in the know'. Many of the practices and norms in therapy that can be immensely puzzling to clients, such as the client and therapist not having a concurrent social relationship, have good ethical foundations and make sense to clients if they are explained.

Taking time to explain your therapeutic approach (and any alternative approaches that might be available) in a way that makes sense to your client is crucial. It is likely, however, that your client, whoever they are and wherever they are from, will not really understand what it is you do until they have some experience of actually working with you. It is important that clients are not encouraged to end prematurely just because therapy is unfamiliar to them. I was once told by a client who arrived with no idea as to why he had been referred, and no familiarity with therapy when we began, that we couldn't stop when we reached the last of our allotted sessions because he'd only just worked out what to do with me (we found a way of transitioning into long-term work).

Worlds apart

All therapeutic approaches are inevitably embedded in the worldview of the society in which they develop. The essential characteristics of your therapeutic approach will invariably be, to some degree, culture-specific, as will some of the more peripheral ideas associated with it. There is, for instance, much made of the individualism of humanist therapies that were developed in the USA. In the literature, this individualism is often set against the collectivism of 'Eastern cultures', and it is claimed that people in 'the East' see themselves as members of a family or wider community rather than as individuals and that relational harmony is valued over personal freedom.

There is much that is useful in making such contrasts and, as discussed later in this chapter, much that is problematic. On the positive side, it may, for example, be potentially useful to understand that an international student brought up within a system of filial piety and a student counsellor who sees university as an opportunity for young people to learn how to be independent may have very different values in relation to family relationships. It is important to develop an increasing awareness that your own worldview and the worldview implied by your therapeutic approach, are not universally shared.

> **Case study**
>
> Sally's client Dayita was in a quandary after some colleagues invited her to go on a week's holiday with them. She wanted to go, but was reluctant to leave her family. Sally suggested that, at 19 and 21, her children could, perhaps, manage without her. She gently challenged Dayita's intention to ask her husband's permission by asking how it would be to make her own decision.
>
> Dayita thought it would be selfish. She was constantly appalled by the way white people just did what they wanted without thinking about others, the way they neglected each other and the way that the parents and children spoke to each other. She knew perfectly well that her children were competent adults and it was obvious that they could obviously manage without her – but she knew that they would miss her and would be hurt if she did not ask how they would feel about her being away. She also knew that she would miss them.
>
> Nor was she, as Sally suggested, 'giving her power away' to her husband. He always asked her permission – and the children's permission – before going away to a conference that he did not absolutely have to go to. When his daughter had objected to the prospect of him being away on her ninth birthday, he had not gone. It irritated her that Sally always seemed to see 'power issues' where she saw respect, care, love and decency. Dayita did not say any of this. She had tried challenging Sally's views before and been treated to a series of silly slogans. Dayita understood what Sally was trying to say, and she understood the values that underpinned her thinking. She just wished that this understanding worked both ways.

Advice giving

Two very influential writers in the cross-cultural therapy literature, Derald Wing Sue and David Sue (2016) argue that clients from cultures that value communality are likely to expect advice – and that they should be given it. They suggest that clients from some ethnic communities, specifically 'Asians', such as Dayita, will expect a therapist to be more like a doctor or priest, and that refraining from advice giving will alienate them. They also suggest that clients who are poor are likely to be concerned with basic survival and so need advice and immediate solutions. They argue that refraining from advice giving is in line with the individualistic values of Western therapy and at odds with cultures that value interdependence.

Unfortunately, their various lines of argument potentially add up to clients who are racially or ethnically 'different', or poor, being offered paternalistic relationships in which they are essentially told what to do, while white, middle-class clients are offered a more egalitarian relationship. This, of course, is not Sue and Sue's intent, but is nevertheless a risk. The most impoverished and socially disadvantaged clients that I have worked with are among those who seem to gain the most from having a safe space in which they felt valued and understood, and in which they could talk freely.

Many clients who are new to therapy expect advice, whatever their social status. But therapy and advice giving are two very different activities. If a client needs legal, financial or some other sort of practical advice, you should, of course, help them access this. Advice about more personal issues is something else entirely. In many cultures this more personal kind of advice is understood as something that you have a right to expect from someone who is supposed to help you. Theorists, such as Sue and Sue recommend advice giving on that basis, but what they fail to mention is that giving this kind of advice comes with a great deal of responsibility. In many communities, if the advice you give turns out to be bad advice, you are (in theory, at least) responsible for putting things right.

Bad advice can also damage relationships. Advice giving is a high-risk activity at the best of times. The risk becomes exponentially higher if a client is from a culture, or subculture, that you are not intimately familiar with. I've lost count of the number of times that supervisees have told me that a previous supervisor has told them that a client 'just needs to be more assertive' in contexts in which assertiveness is likely to backfire quite badly.

Case study

Meena, a 24-year-old Pakistani-Scot, wanted to go for a weekend away with her university friends and guessed that her parents, with whom she lived, would not be enthusiastic. Carole, her first therapist, tried to help her become more assertive. Meena knew that the bluntness of the phrases that Carole suggested would not only backfire, but would also hurt and alarm her parents, so she went to see Paul, a 'culture-affirming' therapist.

Paul was keen to help her find helpful resources from within her own community. He suggested that she ask her brother to go with her so that her parents would feel that they had satisfied their duty to protect her. Meena found her brother's silent but palpable judgment of her friends irritating and embarrassing and knew that his presence would make her (and her friends) feel self-conscious and uncomfortable.

Ruth, the third therapist she saw, said, 'They're your parents. You know what they respond to'. Meena did indeed know. She knew how to prepare them by dropping hints. She knew when and how to respectfully ask their permission. She knew how to reassure them of her safety, and how to wait patiently while they thought about it. After some deliberation, they eventually said yes – and she didn't have to take a chaperone.

A little knowledge is a dangerous thing

Individualism versus collectivism is not the only polarity attributed to 'The West' and 'The East'. Drawing on several other authors, Suki Bassey and Steve Melluish (2013) attribute 19 different orientations and values to 'Western cultures' or 'Eastern cultures'. These include problem solving versus contemplation, mind–body distinction versus mind–body unity, free will versus determinism, and informality versus formality. While often accompanied with a warning that they should not be used to stereotype, these broad claims about entire countries or continents inevitably do exactly that.

There is some truth in the idea that particular values are promoted by particular societies, but it is, as the novelist Sathnam Sanghera (2013) says, also the case that whatever is said about any culture, the opposite can usually be said too. Rather than making individualism, for instance, the property of 'the West' and communality the property of 'the East', it is perhaps more useful to see people in both 'The West' and 'The East' – and those who inhabit both – as moving back and forth on a continuum between self-concern and concern for others. It is our job as therapists to be attentive and curious when a client finds such movement difficult.

Case study

Rani, a nurse in a busy inner city hospital, described to me how, on returning from work, she habitually spent a couple of hours alone, rather than with her parents and siblings. She was very worried about this, and thought that there was something wrong with her. I was aware from friendships, as well as from reading, that 'space' in the sense of time alone is a particularly 'Western' concept, but I was also aware that it is not necessarily a peculiarly 'Western' need. The concepts that our culture makes available to us do not encompass all of human experience, and so that experience can be difficult to put into words when a concept is not available to us.

I asked Rani whether, given how hectic work was, she might just need some time alone when she finished. She eyed me with curiosity, and said 'That's it! But why? Why would I need that?'

'There are a lot of people, all wanting your attention when you're at work. Maybe you just need to switch off for a while.'

'But my parents are really hurt. And they're worried about me.'

'Yeah. People who re-energise by being with other people sometimes don't realise that some of us need time alone to recharge. I've got a friend like that. She used to arrive on my doorstep the minute I finished work. But she understood when I explained that I needed an hour or so to change gear.'

Rani talked to her parents about what her day at work was like, and, like my friend, they were able to understand her need for some time alone. The key, I think, was in linking her need to be alone with her busy day. Rani and I had talked about the introvert/extrovert distinction in the (Jungian) sense of introverts needing solitude to recharge, and extroverts needing company, but agreed that using the word 'introvert' might alarm her parents (as it does many, even in supposedly individualistic societies such as the USA).

Conclusion

The cross-cultural therapy literature is not alone in making sweeping generalisations about large groups of people. We would do well to learn from the public outrage over a transcultural nursing textbook which contained a brief guide to the way culture influences patients' response to pain and included statements such as: 'Muslim clients must endure pain as a sign of faith', 'Blacks often report higher pain intensity' and 'Jews may be vocal and demanding' (Pearson, 2015). Sierra Lawson and Steven Ramey (2018) call these authoritative generalisations 'simplified knowledge'. They found that some of these statements do appear in the research papers that the textbook references, but that the author of the book omitted qualifiers (such as 'many' or 'some'), did not account for the limitations of the research projects, inappropriately generalised conclusions about very specific groups of people to entire racial and ethnic groups, and did not acknowledge contradictory research results within or among research projects.

Contradictions and inconsistencies within and among research results do not lead to a reliable way of predicting how members of a group will behave – and that, Lawson and Ramey conclude, is precisely the point. The authoritative generalisations that constitute simplified knowledge fail to convey the complexity of communities – or to invite us to wonder who produced this 'knowledge' and in what context. Authoritative generalisations about the values and communication styles of huge groups of people abound in the literature on cross-cultural therapy – and should be approached with great caution. The next chapter suggests alternative reading material that can support developing cultural awareness and your professional and personal development more generally.

Further reading

How psychological distress may be experienced elsewhere

Head, B. (1974) *A Question of Power*. Exeter: Heinemann.
Littlewood, R. and Dein, S. (2013) '"Islamic fatalism": Life and suffering among Bangladeshi psychiatric patients and their families in London – an interview study', *Anthropology & Medicine*, 20(3): 264–77.

Resources on counselling and psychotherapy throughout the world

Marks, S. (2018) 'Suggestion, persuasion and work: Psychotherapies in communist Europe', *European Journal of Psychotherapy & Counselling*, 20(1): 10–24.
Martin, K. (2018) 'Transcultural histories of psychotherapy', *European Journal of Psychotherapy & Counselling*, 20(1): 104–19.
Moodley, R., Gielen, U. and Wu, R. (2013) *Handbook of Counseling and Psychotherapy in an International Context*. Abingdon: Routledge.
Pols, H. (2018) 'Towards trans-cultural histories of psychotherapies', *European Journal of Psychotherapy & Counselling*, 20(1): 88–103.
Shamdasani, S. (2018) 'Towards transcultural histories of psychotherapies', *European Journal of Psychotherapy & Counselling*, 20(1): 4–9.

7
Cultural Humility

'Or shall we meet at your place?'

Learning aims

- To appreciate 'culture' as a complex phenomenon about which one cannot amass 'facts'.
- To develop cultural humility.
- To use literary fiction as a resource in working with clients' cultural identities.
- To use literary fiction as a resource in working with clients who have fled atrocities or persecution.

The previous chapter found fault with simplified knowledge as a means of learning about your client's context. This chapter invites cultural humility by encouraging a realistic appreciation of 'culture' as a complex phenomenon about which one cannot amass 'facts'. It suggests reading othered writers as a means of developing an appropriate background familiarity with a client's context and recommends specific writers.

> **Reflective exercise**
>
> Depending on whether you are doing this exercise on your own or with others, think, write or talk about what a therapist from elsewhere would need to know about your culture in order to work with you in a culturally sensitive manner.

There are a number of reasons as to why you may have found the exercise above difficult. You will, for instance, be unaware (as we all are) of a great many of the ways in which your culture shapes your perception and your experience. You may also have a more complex identity than that suggested by your nationality alone. We all live within many cultures, or, to put it another way, we experience our culture from a particular position depending on our gender, class, religion, sexual identity and age. 'British culture' will mean one thing to an elderly upper middle-class lady in the Home Counties, and quite another to a 15-year-old working-class girl in Tyneside.

You might have found the above exercise complicated because you reject or do not identify with some of your culture's worldviews or values – or identify more strongly with a subculture. If, for instance, you are gender neutral, it would probably be important to you that your imaginary therapist understands that you experience gender in a very different way to that presented by the media, medical profession and other cultural institutions. Most clients have at least some ambivalence towards aspects of their culture, or at some point struggle with social constraints and expectations. Cultural values influence rather than dictate personal values.

Real clients usually live within a complex of many cultures and subcultures. They both embody and struggle with and against their various cultural values as the following case study shows.

> **Case study**
>
> Dennis is, by day, a young but already well-respected member of a community known for its homophobia and, by night, a fixture of the gay club scene. His parents are gently pressuring him to marry a woman from his community whom he has been dating for a couple of years. His gay friends are equally gently pressuring him to come out. He had, when he started therapy, already decided not to risk his community and family relationships by coming out. But he did find living in two separate worlds simultaneously very stressful. What he benefited from in therapy was having a relationship in which all aspects of who he is were welcomed. Therapy is, for many clients, the only place in which they can hope to integrate what conflicting social pressures demand they separate.

You may even have concluded that it would be preferable for your imaginary therapist to *not* know much about your culture because you want to be free of some of its values or beliefs. Whilst it is important not to ignore or challenge a client's values inappropriately, it is also important to remember that therapy works, in part, because it is to some extent, countercultural. The active ingredient for Freud, for instance, is in giving words to that which is culturally taboo, and for Carl Rogers and Eugene Gendlin it is in accepting and symbolising one's experience despite social pressure to do otherwise.

The possibility that the client might need to push away from 'their culture' in some way is rarely written about (although there is an early body of literature that assumes 'other' cultures are invariably a source of oppression and psychological distress). The anthropologist Arthur Kleinman (1995) argues that people are often placed in very difficult situations in which adhering to a culturally endorsed course of action may simply cause too much suffering. That is precisely the kind of dilemma that brings people into therapy.

Becoming sufficiently attuned to your client's worldview in order to be a sensitive companion, make an appropriate intervention or do whatever else it is that you want to do is not a straightforward task. The bottom line is that you cannot understand another's person's culture unless you have lived their life. Culture is not a 'thing'; it does not exist in and of itself, but is enacted, or lived, within relationships. It needs a particular context. It also needs particular people as it is always experienced from a particular position or point of view. It is subjective, and cannot be distilled into objective, generalised knowledge.

Case study

Cultures change with time and place. A supervisee, Durnaz, was a therapist within the Pakistani community in Bradford. After her first session with Effat, a woman who had recently arrived from Pakistan to get married, she spent our supervision session exploring the disconnect between them. Effat, who had run her own business in Pakistan and had a vibrant social life there, was shocked to find that, in Bradford, she could not even leave her house without several neighbours alerting her husband. Effat's expectations of how life in Bradford would be caught Durnaz so off-guard that they had become the focus of their session.

What is current in Lahore or Lagos may be very different to how things are in the Pakistani or Nigerian communities in London or Leeds. Practices change. Beliefs change. Customs fall away and are replaced. What is current in a country will not necessarily be current across its diaspora. So beware of generalisations about 'Nigerian culture' or (worse) 'African culture'.

Traditions are not static or enduring. I used to spend a lot of time with some Indian friends and whenever we went to a party or other largish gathering, the women sat separately from the men. Then that stopped. I don't know what happened, just that 'we're not doing that anymore'. This seems to me to be a more realistic form of cultural 'knowledge' than abstracted generalisations. It comes from a particular position. I am a guest – and my knowledge is limited. I don't know how the decision was made or by whom. There being constraints on what I'm included in reminds me that an Indian client would experience the same situation from a different position, and would be included in some ways, but also excluded in others. There is no universal, general or typical experience of 'a culture', partly because there is no typical person. James Davies (2019) understands culture as something that we *do,* rather than as something that we have. We learn about culture in the doing of it, by being in relationships.

Listening to the 'other'

We can also learn about how culture may be 'done', in various contexts, by listening to what the 'other' has to say about themselves. Some therapists that I have spoken to have a preference for autobiography, memoir and journalism because they are about real people. Those who are sceptical that reading something made-up can be helpful in understanding an actual client may be surprised to know that there is 'hard' (i.e. experimental) evidence that it can.

David Kidd and Emanuele Castano (2013) found that literary fiction helps us develop an understanding of other people, and is better at doing so than non-fiction (or genre fiction, or not reading at all). They suggest that this is because literary fiction is peopled by complicated characters whose inner lives are not easily discerned, and so engage our ability to theorise or infer thoughts, feelings, motivations and other psychological processes. Our everyday social experiences are, they argue, informed by convention and stereotypes, which literary fiction disrupts and challenges.

I would add to this that literary fiction also gives us a privileged understanding of several viewpoints and psychological processes: the author's, the narrator's and multiple characters. Neither the author, the narrator, nor any of the characters will be the same as your client, but they all communicate something of your client's context. They aid our imagination, our ability to understand that which is beyond our own experience. The case studies in this book are fictionalised (I have added fictional details as well as removing real and identifying details) in order to uphold confidentiality, but, hopefully, still useful.

Fiction written by writers from other countries or from marginalised groups is a particularly useful resource for therapists seeking to understand the 'other'. It gives us access to the 'other's' voice. It invites us in to 'their' worlds. It allows us to inhabit other spaces, to become familiar with sights, smells, dust, noise, to imagine a different landscape, a different life. Listening to the voices of the 'other' gives us a foundation from which to engage theory of mind (Premack and Woodruff, 1978), to empathise, to understand the 'other' in their own terms.

> **Case study**
>
> I, for instance, found Ismail Kadare's novel *Broken April* (1978) incredibly helpful when working with Idris, an ethnic Albanian boy who had fled the war in Kosovo. The Home Office wanted to return him to his extended family in Albania. He was insistent that if he returned, he would kill his cousin in revenge for another murder within the family. When I enquired as to how Idris felt about this death and how he felt about his cousin, he said that he hadn't liked the dead guy anyway, but loved his cousin like a brother. I was not unfamiliar with honour killings in other communities. This seemed very different. There was no passion, no rage, no wounded feelings.
>
> I did some research in an effort to understand the emotional context. I read newspaper reports about the Albanian social code, *Kunan*, which includes honour killing, making a comeback in some parts of post-communist Albania. But it was only when I happened to read *Broken April* that I finally understood that revenge killing is a social obligation that has nothing to do with what the killer feels or wants.

Fiction, autobiography, memoir and journalism are all potentially helpful in understanding culture-specific practices like this from within the lives of those who embody – and wrestle – with them. But it is also important to have some sense of how a client might experience that which is also familiar to us. In a deliciously satirical essay on how to write about Africa, Binyavanga Wainaina (2006) says that ordinary domestic scenes, references to African writers or intellectuals, and school-going children who are not suffering from Ebola or female genital mutilation are taboo. His memoir, *One Day I Will Write About This Place* (Wainaina, 2011), is an account of an ordinary, un-dramatic, well-fed, middle-class African childhood and young adulthood. There is no sensationalism, just really wonderful writing.

Writing that sensationalises makes the 'other' an object of our projections. Fiction that is written by 'them' to explain 'their people' to 'us' can also be distancing (and is often very dated). Fiction that does not burden itself with this demand, but does provide an insider's account in which the 'other' takes centre stage, welcomes us into 'their' homes, lives and families unselfconsciously. Rohinton Mistry's *Family Matters* (2003) invites us into the home and life of a family in present-day Mumbai. Tishani Doshi also writes about family, drawing upon her parents' Indian–Welsh marriage in *The Pleasure Seekers* (2010). Rohinton's family (both in the novel and in his own life) is Parsi, and Doshi's is Jain, and so the characters in the two novels do 'Indian culture' quite differently, as do the characters in Sathnam Sanghera's *Marriage Material,* which is set not in India, but in the Sikh community in Birmingham. Jhumpa Lahiri's *The Namesake* (2003) is immensely helpful in understanding why Indians use different names in different contexts, and what this means.

There is an abundance of other really good contemporary South Asian and South-Asian origin novelists writing in English, including Kamila Shamsie and Nadeem Aslam (Pakistan), Preti Tanega, Arundhati Roy, Anuradha Roy, Nikesh Shukla, Anita Desai and Sunjeev Sahota (India), Tahmima Anam (Bangladesh), Khaled Hosseini (Afghanistan), Ru Freeman (Sri Lanka) and Jhumpa Lahiri (West Bengal). Some of their works are set in South Asian countries or South Asian communities in Britain, some not. I would recommend them all for the sheer pleasure of reading them. However, Roopa Farooki is perhaps the most obvious resource for therapists. *The Good Children* (2014) is an insightful exploration of coping (or not) with having been brought up by a narcissistic parent.

There is also an abundance of really good contemporary Nigerian and Nigerian-origin novelists writing in English. Other than Chinwa Achebe, the best-known are Ben Okri and Chimamanda Ngozi Adichie, but Helen Oyeyemi, Bernardine Evaristo, Sefi Atta, Ayòbámi Adébáyò, Adaobi Tricia Nwaubani, Titilola Alexandrah Shoneyin and Olumide Popoola are also very much worth reading. Popoola's *When we Speak of Nothing* (2017) is a particularly useful resource for therapists working with young people, or with clients who were young, black and living in London at the time of the riots following the death of Mark Duggan.

Sadly there is no space to recommend appropriate novels from all the countries from which you are most likely to see a client (if you work in higher education that could be almost every country in the world). I will, however, recommend some Caribbean authors in recognition of those who were so abused by the Home Office during the Windrush scandal.

Novelists such as Sam Selvon and George Lamming who were writing in the 1950s are well known for writing about the experience of emigrating to England, as the contemporary novelist Andrea Levy does in *Small Island* (2004). Other contemporary novelists explore the political situations that encouraged emigration. Marlon James's *A Brief History of Seven Killings* (2014), which spans several decades in Jamaica up to and including the 1990s, is a notoriously difficult, if enlightening read. Margaret Cezair-Thompson's *The True History of Paradise* (1999) whose backdrop is the Jamaican State of Emergency in Easter 1981, is much easier to read and speaks to the haste and regret of so many people in so many countries who feel that they have no option but to leave.

I earlier summarised Prossy Kakoozan (Kakoozan in conversation with Boyles, 2017) as saying that it was important to her, as a client, that her therapist understood something of the social and political context from which she had fled. Journalistic accounts that give the facts, and also something of the emotional and psychological realities, such as Alia Malek's *The Home that was our Country: A Memoir of Syria* (2017), may be particularly helpful. Leaving horrific circumstances behind is often only the beginning of an immensely difficult journey without a safe end. Behrouz Boochani's *No Friend but the Mountains: Writing from Manus Prison* (2018) is dystopian in its analysis of how the Australian immigration system dehumanises those who seek its protection. He wrote it via text messages while imprisoned.

Like this kind of journalism, fiction can give us a human context in which to understand the facts, or rather political perspectives, of a conflict from which a client has sought refuge. Some clients need to process traumatic events that they have lived through in the past, as Aminatta Forna does in *The Devil that Danced on the Water* (2002) or Hisham Matar (2016) in *The Return: Fathers, Sons and the Land in Between*. Both are trying to process and understand the politically motivated deaths of their fathers, Forna's in Sierra Leone in the decades leading up to the bloodshed of the 1990s and Matar's in Libya in 1990.

Fiction that is set during conflicts that were not current during your lifetime, or which you did not understand at the time, and perhaps still do not understand, can be a really useful resource when working with clients affected by those conflicts. Obviously the stories of the characters in a novel are not your client's story, but having a broad context in which to understand your client's story is immensely important in developing a good enough understanding.

Chimamanda Ngozi Adichie's (2006) *Half of a Yellow Sun* is set between 1960 and 1970, and gives an account of the Biafran war told mainly through the eyes of Igbo characters. It is harrowing, as is Maaza Mengiste's (2010) *Beneath the Lion's Gaze*, which is invaluable reading for therapists who need to understand what it is like to live through extreme political repression, and/or who want to understand the Ethiopian revolution. Mengiste provides a lengthy bibliography of historical resources for those who prefer non-fictionalised accounts or who want to read further. Kader Abdolah's (2010) *The House of the Mosque* follows the lives of its characters through the period before, during and after the Iranian revolution of 1979. A young woman lets go of her dream of corrective facial surgery as ordinary life ebbs away during the 1990s economic sanctions imposed on Iraq following the Gulf War in Betool Khedairi's *Absent* (2007).

Clients who have lived through traumatic events as children need their therapist to understand how these events might be experienced by a child. Ru Freeman's (2013) *On Sal Mal Lane* is written largely from the perspective of a group of siblings watching ordinary life slip away as conflict between the Sinhalese government and Tamil Tigers erupts in Sri Lanka in the 1980s. Hisham Matar's (2006) *In the Country of Men*, set in Gaddafi's Libya and Gael Faye's (2016) *Small Country,* set in Burundi as war is breaking out there and in Rwanda in 1992, are particularly painful accounts of what children understand, and what they do not understand. Uzodinma Iweala's (2005) *Beasts of No Nation* is written from the point of view of a child soldier.

Fiction can portray – and, more importantly, evoke – the emotional realities that facts do not necessarily take us to. It gives us a particularly privileged insight into the emotional and psychological realities of ordinary people in extreme situations. Louise Burns's (2018) *The Milkman* and Sulaiman Addonia's (2018) *Silence is my Mother Tongue* both evoke the suffocating scrutiny with which one is watched in traumatised communities. *The Milkman* is set in Northern Ireland in the 1970s and *Silence is my Mother Tongue* in a refugee camp – Addonia lived in a refugee camp in Sudan and arrived in the UK as an unaccompanied child.

Fiction may use artistic licence with regard to some of the facts, but it has a unique ability to help us see, hear, smell, touch, taste and feel. It engages our senses and our emotions. When a client has been through the unimaginable, it is our job to imagine. But it is important to remember that even when imagining the world of the 'other', we understand it from our own perspective. It was important for Kakoozan (Kakoozan in conversation with Boyles, 2017) that her therapist did not use their background knowledge to make assumptions about her feelings. If you read any of the novels recommended above, you will certainly have your own emotional responses to the events described – and you will also have access to the perhaps quite different responses of the characters. Fiction increases our ability to empathise, to enter into emotional worlds that may be quite different to our own and to appreciate that one person's experience of a situation will not be the same as another person's experience of the same situation.

Literary fiction, like therapy, is concerned with that which is complex, subjective, contradictory, unspoken, silenced. It gives access to multiple points of view, and provides a space for the criticism and even rejection of social values and practices (which is why it is often banned in totalitarian states). Therapy (which also tends to be banned in totalitarian states) should provide a similar space. Clients are not representatives of 'their culture', but people doing their best from within a complex network of social and political forces.

It is for this reason that one should beware of believing that there is a particular way of working with clients that are perceived as belonging to a particular group. Some therapeutic traditions have begun to adapt or modify their ways of working so as to make them more appropriate to specific cultural groups. This approach becomes problematic when it uses simplified knowledge. However, it need not do so.

Family therapists Jessica Binkley and Shahana Koslofsky (2017), for instance, do not suggest that a particular 'adaptation' should be used with all clients from a perceived group. Instead, they emphasise the importance of the practitioner continually monitoring how their own marginalised and privileged identities impact upon the therapeutic work. They warn against preconceptions based on cultural judgments (and to this one might add preconceptions based upon cultural ignorance). They emphasise the importance of differences within perceived groups and warn against 'cultural errors' such as stereotyping or assuming there are cultural factors at play where there are not and ignoring them when they are. Binkley and Koslofsky obtained the cultural information that they needed to do the work described in their paper by consulting a colleague from the client's ethnic group. It matters that they were able to ask for guidance in relation to that specific client and their unique context.

Hubert and Stuart Dreyfus (1986) tell us that skilful performance, or what, in this context, might be better thought of as professional wisdom, is developed not through abstract principles, but through many experiences, all of which happen in specific contexts. It is perhaps for this reason that reading about particular characters in particular contexts can help us attune to the unique individuals with whom we work.

> **Case study**
>
> A client whom I had seen only once before was again talking about her family, but seemed to be describing an entirely different family to the one she had talked about the previous week. It transpired that she was indeed talking about another family. As she described being 'given' to this other family and growing up in their household, I realised that she was telling me that she had grown up as a servant, possibly an unpaid servant. Fortunately, I was simultaneously aware that explicitly saying so would be shaming. She looked at me quizzically. I nodded and indicated that I'd understood. We moved on and said no more about it until she had grounds to decide that our relationship was safe enough.
>
> Both my awareness that children are, for a variety of reasons, sometimes 'given' to a distant relative or to the family of a privileged member of the community, and my awareness that in many contexts, this is both perfectly ordinary and also a potential source of shame, came from reading novels. I did not, in the moment, remember any specific books or characters. Rather, it seemed as if I remembered an emotional atmosphere. This atmosphere of lowliness, being an outsider, sleeping on the kitchen floor is not from my own life but something I have breathed in as novelists have brought me to unfamiliar places and thrown me into intimate relationships with people who never existed.

Conclusion

Ignorance of other cultures is inevitable – and not the real problem. The real problem in trying to understand 'their culture' is arrogance. Melanie Tervalon and Jann Murray-Garcia (1998) criticise the idea that 'cultural competence' can be reached by learning a finite body of knowledge, and suggest that it be replaced with the idea of cultural humility. They emphasise the importance of being flexible enough to relinquish the false sense of security that stereotyping brings and of being willing to learn about each client from that client.

We can only ever really understand a culture in which we have lived, as an insider, for a long time; preferably including childhood. In other words, we can only ever truly understand our own culture(s), and even then only from our own social position. It is more realistic to try to identify the culturally determined lens through which we ourselves understand the world. The problem with this very sensible aim is that it is very difficult to see the worldview in which we are steeped. It is difficult to differentiate our perception unless we look from a different perspective. The paradoxical answer to this problem is that it is in looking at the world through another's eyes that we become aware of how we see it. Listening to the voice of the 'other' allows us to see the world through 'their' eyes, and in doing so we become aware that our own perspective is simply a perspective. 'We' do not have a monopoly on reality, and neither do our therapeutic approaches.

Further reading

BPS (2018) *Guidelines for Psychologists Working with Refugees and Asylum Seekers in the UK: Extended Version*. Available at: www.bps.org.uk/sites/bps.org.uk/files/Policy/Policy%20-%20Files/Guidelines%20for%20Psychologists%20Working%20With%20Refugees%20and%20Asylum%20Seekers%20in%20the%20UK%20-%20Extended%20%28Update%20Nov%202018%29.pdf (accessed 12 September 2019).

As I have already recommended a lot of novels in this chapter, these recommendations concern film rather than literature.

Bhugra, D. (2003) 'Using film and literature for cultural competence training', *Psychiatric Bulletin*, 27(11): 427–8.

Frick, M.H., Thompson, H. and Curtis, R. (2017) 'Using films to increase cultural competence in working with LGBTQ clients', *The Journal of Counselor Preparation and Supervision*, 9(2): 1–28.

8
Demonising and Romanticising the 'Other'

'Your place is so far away!'

Learning aims

- To consider the possibility that you may sometimes either demonise or romanticise 'their culture'.
- To consider, as an example, the ways in which 'their culture' is demonised by the larger political narrative on female genital mutilation (FGM).
- To engage with some difficult ethical questions with regard to professional guidelines on FGM.

The idea that ethnic groups have distinct and identifiable cultures was invented by the anthropologist Edward Burnett Tylor in 1871. Obviously different societies had always eaten, spoken, danced, brought up children, meted out justice and healed each other in particular ways. What Tylor introduced was the idea that these ways could be observed and codified, an idea rejected by contemporary anthropologists who see this idea of culture as implying that 'traditions' are enduring, when in reality they change as they are practised, ignored, forgotten or returned to.

New understandings of culture are emerging that are 'experience-near' and look at the actual practice of real lives rather than constructing the sorts of grand theories that so often end up presented as simplified knowledge. As discussed in the previous chapter, the idea that culture is something that we *do* rather than something that we 'have', that it is something that is brought into being by being enacted in relationships, is particularly useful in a therapeutic context.

The contemporary feminist anthropologist Lila Abu-Lughod (1991) sees the concept of culture as not only oversimplifying and stereotyping the 'other', but as the tool with which the 'other' is constructed. The very idea that someone is from a 'different culture', she argues, invites us to see them as 'other'. The dangers of simplified knowledge have already been discussed in previous chapters. This chapter invites you to examine whether you also use the whole notion of culture in an inappropriately simplistic way.

The notion of the 'other' and 'their culture' is often used to split off and project onto 'them' that which we deny in ourselves. The chapter begins by inviting you to look at how the national narrative on female genital mutilation does this, and what the implications are for therapeutic practice. Although the most easily recognised form of projecting is demonisation, romanticising and exoticising the 'other' is also unhelpful. The chapter ends by discussing the risks when, as strongly encouraged in some of the cross-cultural therapy literature, working collaboratively with traditional healers.

'Their culture'

> **Reflective exercise**
>
> Your 15-year-old client is due to be married in her country of origin. She tells you, with coy excitement, that she will be 'made smoother and tighter' before she gets married. This will involve having her labia cut, scraped, and joined together to form a seal over part of her vagina. She laughs at your reaction and says that many of her friends from home have had this done and that, apart from the after-pain, she is looking forward it.
>
> Before you read further, imagine how you might respond to what this client has told you.

The client in the above exercise is from the USA, where the procedures that she intends to undergo are not called 'female genital mutilation', but are known as 'genital cosmetic surgery', specifically 'labiaplasty' and 'laser vaginal rejuvenation' – or, as the client puts it, 'a Barbie'. The language that 'we' use constructs what are very similar procedures – and the women and girls on whom they are performed – very differently depending on whether they are performed in the global south and its diaspora (victims of mutilation) or in the global north (consumers of cosmetic surgery). Many women from the global south find the term 'mutilation' deeply offensive and prefer 'circumcision' or 'cutting'.

Wherever they are performed, these procedures have no medical purpose. They are performed for cultural reasons in both the global south *and* the global north. Someone who has her labia or clitoral hood surgically 'reduced' because she thinks them ugly, because she wants to emulate a porn aesthetic (Schick et al., 2011) or to avoid a 'camel toe' is clearly subject to cultural pressures (cosmetic surgeons actually do give the avoidance of 'camel toe' as a valid reason for these procedures – see, for instance, www.altermd.com/clitoropexy_clitoral_hood_reduction.htm). But these pressures are invisible to those immersed in that culture. Many in the global south believe that circumcision keeps a girl clean. Many people in the global north believe the same thing about male circumcision, which is why it is so common for American boys to be circumcised even when there is no medical or religious imperative to do so. Both are cultural beliefs.

The government has taken the position that female genital mutilation (FGM) is *not* a cultural practice, but child abuse (this applies only to female, not male, circumcision). Defining FGM as child abuse (Parliament, House of Commons, 2014) enables the law to punish anyone who performs a medically unnecessary, painful and potentially dangerous procedure on a child. However, there is a convincing argument that legislation does not stop FGM, which is illegal in many of the countries in which it is commonly practised, but instead drives it underground. FGM is a community practice. Women who are not circumcised may be thought disgusting and shunned. Parents who decide not to have their daughters cut in a community in which it is usual are likely to be under intense pressure to change their minds for their daughters' sake.

Legislation seems to be of little effect against the will of a community, but education does make a difference. The first conviction for FGM in the UK was in February 2019, when the mother of a three-year-old was sent to prison and the child and her brother removed from their family. The social activist and survivor of FGM, Leyla Hussein, told *The Guardian* newspaper (Summers and Ratcliffe, 2019) that teachers, health professionals and the whole system had failed to protect this child by not educating her mother. Hussein had chosen not to have her own daughter circumcised after a nurse raised the issue with her and had given her the information that she'd needed to make that choice.

The problem with conceptualising female circumcision as child abuse is that it criminalises parents who want to do what is best for their daughters in a specific set of circumstances. The practice is unlikely to change on a large scale until resources enable these circumstances to change, and allow parents to imagine and work for a different future for their daughters. If marriage is their daughter's only viable choice, her parents are obliged to make sure that their daughter is marriageable. If decently-paid work is a viable option, they can afford to make a decision that may displease the community but will not put their daughter at risk of a financially insecure future.

Rather than understanding these parents as trying to act in their daughters' long-term interests, the current discourse around FGM not only portrays them as criminals, but, to use a term from a government paper, 'barbaric' (Parliament, House of Commons, 2014). The sentiment of this rather colonialist language is echoed throughout the public discourse on FGM, with one observer at the 2019 trial mentioned above (Berer, 2019) criticising the Crown Prosecution Service for making a spurious link between FGM and witchcraft. The Association of African Women for Research and Development criticise the 'new crusaders' against FGM for their use of sensationalism, and their insensitivity to the dignity of the very women they want to 'save' (Davies, 1983).

The social imagery in relation to genital cosmetic surgery (GCS) is very different. Clinical. Surgical. Expensive. In some countries in the global south – Egypt, for example – much of the female circumcision that happens is performed in hospital by a surgeon, but this is rarely acknowledged in the discourse of outrage. Hospital-provided female circumcision would not be possible in Britain (although it would be possible in Australia, for example, where a symbolic 'nick' is legal). All procedures that cut or pierce a woman or girl's genitalia without medical justification are illegal in Britain, regardless of age. Yet there is no age limit for GCS in Britain and a British doctor has made public her concerns about girls as young as nine being referred for cosmetic labiaplasty.

The Royal College of Midwives (Parliament, House of Commons, 2014) has pointed out the hypocrisy of telling African women to stop a practice that is freely permitted in Harley Street. Medical ethicists who consider genital cosmetic surgery to be unethical also asked the government to clarify its legal status. After some prevarication, during which there was stunned disbelief within the piercing community, and protests by angry young white women, the government decided that it 'does not accept that FGM being forced on a girl in Sierra Leone and genital surgery taking place in Harley Street (or elsewhere) are the same issue. FGM is child abuse, whereas there can be genuine therapeutic reasons for genital surgery' (Parliament, House of Commons, 2015).

But the law on FGM is not about force, or age, and it already makes exception for genuine therapeutic reasons (including gender transition). GCS is, by definition, performed for purely cosmetic reasons – and at a skyrocketing rate. The government's response to The Royal College of Midwives (Parliament, House of Commons, 2015) does not specifically refer to cosmetic surgery, other than to say that the term 'cosmetic' is sometimes used to refer to surgery that is medically necessary (i.e. the word is sometimes misused). The question of whether professionals should apply the law equally, regardless of culture, is unclear and potentially affects therapists as well as midwives.

In 2016, the NHS commissioned The British Association for Counselling and Psychotherapy (BACP) to conduct a survey to gauge its members' awareness and understanding of FGM. Although therapists are under no legal obligation to report FGM, the subsequent report emphasises safeguarding duties (which do apply to psychologists, and other regulated professionals in England and Wales). It is made very clear that the Home Office expects therapists to report FGM even though we are not legally required to do so. The government's expectation of us in relation to the client at the beginning of this section who was planning to have a 'Barbie' in the USA is still unclear – and seems to differ depending on whether the client is white or, for instance, Somali-American.

> **Reporting FGM**
>
> Counsellors and psychotherapists are under no legal obligation to report FGM, but are expected to do so. The following is summarised from the *Home Office's Mandatory Reporting of Female Genital Mutilation – Procedural Information* (2016), which is the guidance for registered professionals, such as psychologists and teachers, in England and Wales.
>
> - The duty to report applies to a direct disclosure made (to you) by a girl under eighteen that she has been cut. It does not apply if an older girl or a woman tells you that she was cut whilst under eighteen.
> - If you are the first professional to be told, you have to make the report yourself – you cannot pass the responsibility on to a colleague or other professional.
> - The report should be made to the client's local police force as soon as possible. Best practice is for reports to be made by the close of the next working day, unless this is likely to put your client or another child at risk or you want to consult your supervisor or other colleagues. Your priority should be your client's safety.
> - In making your report, you should say that you are reporting FGM, although not legally obliged to do so. You should give your name; work telephone number and e-mail address; times when you will be available to speak on the phone; details of your organisation's designated safeguarding lead if applicable and their contact details (and your name, age or date of birth and address).
> - Keep records of your discussions, decisions and actions.
> - The protocol is to inform the child's family. Her family should be told why the report was necessary and what it is likely to mean. You should not have this discussion with your client's family if you believe that doing so will result in them leaving the country or harming your client.
> - You should expect the police to take action if there is an immediate threat of further harm to your client, and to involve other agencies if there is not. This multi-agency response should consider your client's wider emotional needs, and so you may want to be a part of it. The police will otherwise let you know the outcome of the case and if any safeguarding action was taken.
> - You should continue to work with the client if possible.
> - If someone else tells you that a girl under 18 has been cut, you do not need to tell the police. Instead, you should follow your local safeguarding procedures.

'Your culture is so cool!'

Casting the 'other' as exotic, romantic, desirable may seem very different to casting 'them' as criminally cruel, but both are projections that diminish the 'other'.

There is a difference between respecting and romanticising other cultural practices.

The founder of the academic discipline of Postcolonial Studies, Edward Said (1978), used the term 'Orientalism' to describe a patronising perception of Arab societies as exotic. Orientalism exaggerates difference and allows 'us' to be fascinated by 'their culture', while also considering it 'primitive', 'backward', less 'developed' or in some other way inferior. Although Said was writing specifically about a perception of the Arab world, the concept of Orientalism can be readily applied to 'our' relationship with other parts of the world. It is particularly evident when looking back at the British Raj.

Romanticising and venerating simplistic versions of 'other cultures', particularly 'Eastern spirituality', is a more modern form of Orientalism that appears to look up to the 'other' rather looking down on 'them', but actually looks right past them to a more cinematic version. It is important to be alert to the lure of the romanticised and exoticised when engaging with cross-cultural literature that encourages therapists to engage with 'other' healing systems.

Some of this literature encourages therapists to incorporate elements of traditional healing systems into their therapeutic work. Given the title, it is striking that almost none of the many contributors to Moodley and West's (2005) *Integrating Traditional Healing Practices into Counselling and Psychotherapy* actually suggest that therapists should attempt to do so. Rather, they warn against plucking practices out of their context, attempting to work in a way that one does not properly understand, or in some other way underestimating the dedicated, immersive training required to practise properly.

The American cultural competencies literature encourages therapists to not be averse to consulting traditional healers or religious and spiritual leaders when appropriate. Again, it is important to recognise and work through any tendency to exoticise when contemplating this. A traditional African healer, promising to help with an array of complaints from infertility to bad luck, set up a practice near my practice a few years ago. I have a long-standing interest in traditional healing systems and so my ears pricked up. What I heard was sobering. My African neighbours were *horrified* by his arrival. Some immediately identified him as a charlatan, some expressed a fear of his practices, most expressed extreme mistrust of his intentions and a desire to not ever cross paths with him. I know how to check out the credentials and trustworthiness of a massage therapist, for instance, but, as my neighbours' reactions reminded me, I do not have the cultural knowledge to competently assess practitioners from other traditions (and I have personally come unstuck a few times because of this). Consult only when appropriate, not to satisfy your inner anthropologist, and with the diligence you would use in choosing anyone else to consult.

Further reading

Kelly, B. and Foster, C. (2012) 'Should female genital cosmetic surgery and genital piercing be regarded ethically and legally as female genital mutilation?', *British Journal of Obstetrics and Gynaecology*, 119: 389–92.

Moran, C. and Lee, C. (2014) 'What's normal? Influencing women's perceptions of normal genitalia: An experiment involving exposure to modified and nonmodified images', *British Journal of Obstetrics and Gynaecology*, 121: 761–6.

Mowat, H., McDonald, K., Dobson, A.S., Fisher, J. and Kirkman, M. (2015) 'The contribution of online content to the promotion and normalisation of female genital cosmetic surgery: A systematic review of the literature', *BMC Women's Health*, 15: 110.

Nnaemeka, O. (2005) *Female Circumcision and the Politics of Knowledge: African Women in Imperialist Discourses*. Westport, CT: Praeger.

9
Power and Prejudice

'I can't see you'

Learning aims

- To understand how stereotypes, prejudice and discrimination are linked.
- To understand different theories about how prejudice arises.
- To understand the concept of modern prejudice.
- To consider your own prejudices.
- To understand the concept of implicit bias.
- To test your own implicit biases.
- To consider how you might address your implicit biases.

The previous chapter discussed how the current social narrative around medically unnecessary genital surgery portrays women from the global south as victims in need of rescue and women from the global north as empowered consumers. This chapter invites you to consider how social narratives may have influenced your perceptions and feelings in relation to othered clients, i.e. how you may have developed prejudices – and what you can do about them. It may be useful to remember that we are *all* immersed in these narratives and to keep in mind your marginalised as well as your mainstream identities while reading this chapter.

Frantz Fanon (1986 [1952]) argues that our psychic architecture fractures when the social relationships and structures that are supposed to provide safety are, instead, the source of attack. Therapy and therapeutic relationship should provide a safe space in which othered clients can recover from social hostility.

If the relationship that we offer also proves to be an unsafe environment, the potential damage is multiplied exponentially.

Clients make themselves vulnerable by talking about the more difficult, painful, shameful and frightening aspects of their lives. The role of client does not confer power. The role of therapist does. We have the power that accumulates from knowing so much about a client who knows so little about us, from being seen as someone who can help, and from actually being someone who can help. In addition, most of us will frequently find ourselves in therapeutic relationships in which we are a socially mainstream therapist in relation to a socially marginalised client. A combination of role power and social power skews the balance of power very much in our favour. With such power comes the responsibility to do no harm. Ensuring that the therapeutic relationships we offer do not replicate the abusive nature of wider social relationships involves examining preconceptions that we hold, consciously or unconsciously, about the 'other'.

Who, me? Implicit prejudice and bias

As discussed in Chapter 2, the constructions of 'race', class, gender, sexuality, youth, old age, middle age, ethnicity, religious identity and culture claim that members of a particular race or class, etc. are like each other and unlike 'us' – and so we tend to see 'them' in this way. This is stereotyping. Stereotypes are cartoon figures that illustrate society's beliefs about the 'other'. They are not all overtly negative. The stereotype of the 'supercrip' (Schalk, 2016) who 'overcomes' their physical limitation to achieve something astounding (or something fairly ordinary), for instance, does not cast disabled people in an overtly negative light. However, it does express the belief that there is something tragic about being physically impaired and supports the image of disabled people as a source of inspiration for 'us', the more fortunate. What it does not do is affirm disabled people as ordinary folk getting on with ordinary lives. Both negative and positive stereotypes are inevitably dehumanising because they are partial and simplistic. They potentially prevent us from seeing clients as they actually are.

Current stereotypes of the 'other' have their roots in abusive relationships that are centuries old. The concept of social imagery (Bloor, 1991) is a useful means of augmenting the idea of stereotypes. When social imagery – the representations we make of the 'other' and the stories we tell about 'them' – becomes institutionalised long enough to shape generations of thinking, it becomes embedded in our worldview. It shapes what we take for granted and fail to question. It shapes our perception – what we think we see.

Reflective exercise

Pick a number of social groups that you do not identify with and are not otherwise familiar with. Write a description of how you think a client from one of these groups would typically present in therapy. What do you imagine that they might

---

> expect from therapy? How do you think they might feel about being in therapy? How do you imagine they might see you and how might they understand your role?
>
> Depending on whether you are working alone or with others, think, write or talk about the ways in which the assumptions you make might impact the way in which you approach the work.

According to the American psychologist Gordon Allport (1954), stereotypes and in- and out-group biases form the cognitive basis for prejudice. In other words, stereotypes + seeing the 'other' as 'not good like us' = prejudice. Although Allport thought that prejudice also has an emotional component, the social psychology research that followed in the wake of *The Nature of Prejudice* very much focused on cognitive processes.

Henri Tajfel's (1969) research expands upon Allport's claim that prejudice relies on our (perfectly normal) tendency to categorise other people in terms of their group membership, rather than seeing them as individuals. In an experiment in which participants were shown lines of varying lengths with the four shortest lines labelled 'A' and the four longest labelled 'B', the participants, when asked to recall the length of the lines, tended to exaggerate the difference between the lengths of the A lines and the B lines, and recalled the lines in the same category as more similar than they actually were. Tajfel concluded that categorising leads to a distortion in judgment. Because thinking in terms of categories (such as 'race', gender, class, etc.) is understood to be a necessary way to save time and cognitive effort when negotiating the social world, Tajfel's work led to the view, researched throughout the 1970s and 1980s, that prejudice and stereotyping are an inevitable, if unfortunate, consequence of how we process information.

When thinking about this tendency to categorise in relation to those who are othered, the point is that 'their' category has been historically constructed as inferior. Demeaning historical narratives about racial 'differences' – the construction of women as physically, mentally and morally inferior to men, other cultures as backward, gay men and lesbians as mentally ill, Muslims and Jews as the dangerous 'other', the economically disadvantaged as lazy and dirty, the old as useless and disabled people as tragic – form the backdrop to present-day interactions and relationships, as do the missing narratives about those who do not easily fit into existing social categories.

One may wholeheartedly reject these narratives and have strong values about respecting and valuing all people regardless of 'race', religion, class, etc., but we are all exposed to covert messages that position 'others' as being of less value, less deserving of respect. These covert messages come to us in countless indirect ways: omissions in the history we are taught; media representations of who should be admired, who feared, who pitied and who ignored. These messages come to all of us, whether they work to our advantage or detriment. Robin DiAngelo (2012) illustrates the power of the covert and of the internalised by acknowledging that while she may tell her daughter that her intellect and character are far more important than her physical appearance, her daughter observes her mother grooming, worrying about her weight and constantly checking her reflection in the mirror. She cannot bring up her daughter to be free of gender socialisation because she is not free of it herself. DiAngelo (2011, 2018) makes much of the useful idea that being influenced by social narratives does not make you a bad person.

Patricia Devine (1989) was among the first researchers to observe that even those whose conscious attitudes are non-discriminatory usually have an unconscious negative bias against marginalised groups. It is difficult to work on one's own unconscious or implicit biases as they are, by definition, outside our awareness. Bringing that which is out of awareness into awareness is the work of therapy, and one of the many reasons that it is essential that therapists have their own therapy. However, it is possible to hide from oneself even in personal therapy.

Fortunately, Devine's work inspired the development of tools that measure unconscious prejudice. Because we are all exposed to negative messages about particular groups, these tools are useful for everyone. Project Implicit, the collaboration between Harvard, the University of Virginia and the University of Washington that developed these tools, found that most of us operate implicit biases – even against the marginalised groups to which we belong.

The tests involve making associations between words, or words and images placed at diagonals. Unfortunately, this can make some dyslexic people go into 'brain freeze'. The box below recommends the full set of the original tests from Project Implicit (some of which are somewhat dated) and also a couple of more dyslexia-friendly variations from the Social Psychology Network.

> **Self-awareness exercise**
>
> Do some implicit bias tests at:
>
> www.understandingprejudice.org/iat/ (these are the more dyslexia friendly) or
>
> https://implicit.harvard.edu/implicit/takeatest.html (there is a fuller set of tests here)
>
> If you do not do the tests, reflect on why you have chosen not to.
> You might want to reflect on your results, or your reasons for not doing the test, in therapy or supervision.

Changing your mind

The implicit bias research is hopeful that implicit biases can be changed. Influenced as it was by the 'cognitive revolution' of the 1960s and 1970s in North

American psychology, this body of literature understands prejudice in cognitive terms and offers cognitive strategies. Devine (1989), for instance, likened the mental activation of automatic stereotypes to a bad habit. The change process that she speculatively theorised involved suppressing and replacing negative stereotypes by consciously thinking about the egalitarian attitudes one holds every time a stereotype comes to mind. Devine speculated that this would develop associations between stereotype structure and personal belief structure and increase the frequency with which personal belief structure was activated when responding to the 'other'.

The laboratory research that followed on from Devine's work largely consisted of having research subjects employ various cognitive tasks – such as mentally creating a counter-stereotype image – before doing an implicit bias test. The results are mixed. Though most show a decrease (e.g. Blair, 2002) in implicit bias, some, worryingly, show an increase (Galinsky and Moskowitz, 2000). Carpenter and Banaji (2001) found that although their research participants were less likely to make stereotypical associations with women after consciously creating counter-stereotypical mental images, they also found that doing so did not change the automatic judgments that their subjects made about women. Most of the researchers express some doubt about translating the laboratory procedures used into real-life strategies.

Devine et al. (2012) have, more recently, researched an intervention involving five overlapping strategies to reduce implicit race bias. These are:

Stereotype replacement: recognising that your response is based on stereotypes; labelling the response as stereotypical; considering how you can avoid such a biased response in the future and eventually responding in unbiased ways.

Counter-stereotypic imaging: challenging the validity of stereotypes by imagining or bringing to mind non-stereotypical qualities or people.

Individuating: getting to know people as individuals rather than making assumptions about them as a member of a marginalised group.

Perspective taking: taking the (imagined) perspective of the 'other'.

Increasing opportunities for contact: seeking out opportunities to relate positively to actual people so that one's stereotyped and biased thinking can be challenged by real life.

Devine's intervention is potentially helpful to therapists who want to address their own implicit biases. All five strategies are particularly amenable to being put into practice in everyday life – but the real-life situations that you learn from should not begin in the therapy room (unless you're the client rather than the therapist). Clients come to therapy for therapy, not as a self-development opportunity for the therapist. If you need to address your own bias, do it in your own time.

> **Reflective exercise**
>
> Depending on whether you are working alone or with others, think, write or talk about how you might use Devine's strategies. Reading writers from othered communities, for example, might enable you to experiment with taking the 'other's' perspective. Chapter 7 recommends a number of writers.

However, Devine's strategies are not enough. As noted earlier, stereotype replacement does not necessarily do away with negative bias. Individuating – seeing someone as an individual rather than as a stereotype – does not necessarily mean that one will individualise all members of their marginalised group, or that one has no bias against that group, as evidenced by the well-worn (and thankfully somewhat dated) protestations that 'I don't think of you as black' or 'but some of my best friends are gay' (and therefore I cannot possibly be racist/homophobic).

Devine and colleagues (Forscher et al., 2017) recently tested the longer-term effects of these strategies, and found that they could *not* be shown to have any long-term effect on either implicit bias or on the intention to behave in non-discriminatory ways. Although the research subjects who participated in the intervention had lower implicit bias scores afterwards, the control subjects did too, suggesting that practice in doing the tests may make it possible to manipulate the results. However, taking the tests did leave participants more aware of prejudice in others and more willing to challenge it. While challenging prejudice in other people is helpful, doing so while being covertly prejudiced yourself is less than ideal, and certainly not sufficient if you are to work with clients from groups against whom you have a bias.

Not just a bad habit

So why might Devine's strategies fail to produce a long-term reduction in prejudice? The answer perhaps lies in her narrow focus on cognitive processes. Although she and several other researchers looked at how guilt might motivate change, they did not take account of emotion as playing a role in the development of prejudice. Prejudice is not passionless and cerebral; it is angry, fearful and often violent. That is what makes it so frightening.

Allport, whose work formed the theoretical basis of Devine's research (and over 400 other studies), *did* acknowledge that emotion plays a part in developing prejudice. Newman and Caldwell (2005) suggest that the researchers who followed him ignored this aspect of his theory because it was based on psychoanalytic thought, and social psychology was by then distancing itself from psychoanalytic thinking.

Although he followed Freud in thinking that prejudice involves projection, Allport used the term 'complementary projection' to differentiate his claim that we project causal traits onto others to make sense of feelings that we are consciously aware of – you must be dangerous because I feel frightened – from Freud's 'direct projection' in which we project feelings that we are unaware of. Both views are potentially useful, as is their shared idea of displaced aggression: taking your frustration out on an innocent bystander – 'kick the cat' syndrome. Both Allport and Freud would agree that blaming the cat conceals the real reasons for our violence, though Allport would understand blaming the cat as justification after the event and Freud as a denial of aspects of oneself. They would agree that our prejudices say more about ourselves than they do about the 'other'.

> ### Self-awareness exercise
>
> Bring to mind a group against whom you have a negative bias. The bias may be one that you have long been aware of, or that you have just discovered through an implicit bias test. You may even be a member of the group.
>
> What do you not like about 'those people'?
>
> Can you see the qualities you have identified as being a part of a group with which you do identify?
>
> Can you identify these qualities within yourself as an individual?

If projection is not an idea that you subscribe to, Tajfel and Turner's (1979) Social Identity Theory might be a useful way of understanding and working with the emotional aspects of your own prejudices. Social Identity Theory proposes that when our membership of a group is significant for us – as our nationality might be during the Olympic Games, for instance – we think of ourselves in terms of the attributes that we share with other group members, and see ourselves as interchangeable with other group members. When we respond to the world in terms of a collective rather than an individual self, our group identity influences what we feel and how we regulate these feelings. You may feel particularly competitive during the Olympic Games, and ecstatic if your country does well. We tend to idealise the group to which we belong in order to bolster our self-image, and may further bolster our self-image by denigrating the 'out-group'. Intergroup Emotions Theory (Mackie et al., 2000) adds the idea that when a group membership is salient or emotionally significant, we are more aware of how something affects our collective rather than our individual self. Of course our assessment of how something will affect the collective self might be wrong, but it is nevertheless the basis of our reaction.

> **Reflective exercise**
>
> Depending on whether you are working alone or with others, think, write or talk about times in which you have felt a strong identification with various social groups to which you belong. Can you spot ways in which other members of that group have tried to intensify or dampen down your feelings through, for example, the media or social media? What makes your group membership salient for you, and when does it recede into the background?

Which of the social groups that you belong to did you choose *not* to think about while doing the above exercise? Why do you think you chose not to think about your membership of those groups?

Conclusion

Implicit bias is understood as an aspect of 'modern' or 'symbolic' prejudice. These terms refer to people who hold egalitarian values, and are ashamed of having thoughts and feelings about the 'other' that contradict their values. Such thoughts and feelings are therefore suppressed, denied or justified. They usually find expression in the microaggressions discussed in Chapter 1.

Implicit biases are closely related to what Stephan and Stephan (1985) call 'intergroup anxiety', the discomfort that arises when in the company of those against whom one has a bias. Intergroup anxiety commonly results in aversive racism, the avoidance of racially marginalised people (an idea that can be readily applied to the avoidance of other marginalised groups). The 'aversive' in aversive racism refers not only to being averse to the company of the 'other' but also to an aversion against being thought prejudiced. Worrying about a client perceiving you as biased may render you less able to be present, less willing to address difficult material, less focused on your client, less boundaried, and distort your view of your client as well as your behaviour towards them. Trawalter et al. (2012) add that being distracted by anxiety or discomfort makes us more likely to use information-processing shortcuts in noticing, understanding and remembering what a client does or says. It makes us less sensitive and less reliable. It also predisposes us to using the very stereotypes we are anxious to avoid.

Recognising and acknowledging biases can be shame-provoking. It is, however, very necessary. The avoidance of both the 'other' and the avoidance of one's own discomfort and guilt maintain prejudice. African American research subjects participating in research by John Dovidio et al. (2010) were aware of subtle facial cues that betrayed unconscious racial bias in white subjects. The white subjects were unaware that they had exposed themselves. A client who is sensitised to hostility, however mild, is likely to know us better than we know ourselves when it comes to how we really feel about them. Prejudice poisons the therapeutic relationship. Honestly addressing one's prejudices is the single most important task in preparing to work with those who are othered.

Further reading

Dalal, F. (2015) 'Prejudice as ideology: The creation of "us" and "them" groups in society and psychoanalysis', *Psychotherapy and Politics International*, 13(3): 182–93.

DiAngelo, R. (2018) *White Fragility: Why it's So Hard for White People to Talk about Racism*. Boston: Beacon Press.

A video from a comedian to lighten the task of facing one's racism:

Tedex Talks (2011) *Jay Smooth: How I Learned to Stop Worrying and Love Discussing Race*. Available at: www.youtube.com/watch?v=MbdxeFcQtaU&app=desktop (accessed 12 September 2019).

10

Power and Privilege

'Don't you know who I am?'

Learning aims

- Understanding that racism, sexism, ableism, queerphobia, and ethnic, religious and class oppression are not mere prejudice.
- Understanding the differences between individual, institutional and systemic oppression.
- Developing a sense of responsibility for addressing institutional racism within the mental health professions.
- Understanding why difference-blindness is not helpful.
- Developing the ability to recognise when a client does not have the same social privileges that you enjoy.
- Assessing your current suitability for working with clients from particular social groups.

The last chapter invited you to examine your own prejudices and biases. This chapter explains why doing so is not enough. You may find it most useful to read this chapter from your mainstream positions.

Unfortunately, addressing one's own prejudices – and/or helping change other people's prejudices – is not enough. Even if every person alive somehow resolved their need to denigrate the 'other', racism, sexism, ableism, queerphobia, and ethnic/religious/class oppression would not just disappear. The problem is not prejudice alone. Being subjected to negative prejudice – someone disliking or judging you because of what rather than who you are – is always unpleasant, but prejudice becomes weaponised when it is combined with the ability to exert power.

Power

This power may lie in the hands of an immigration officer, a police officer, magistrate, doctor – or a therapist. However, institutional discrimination is not only about prejudiced people in powerful positions. Nor does it only happen in institutions that have a culture or even a policy of overt hostility towards particular groups. In reporting on the police's handling of the murder of Stephen Lawrence, Sir William Macpherson (1999), who concluded that the police were institutionally racist, defined institutional racism as a failure to 'provide an appropriate and professional service to people because of their colour, culture or ethnic origin', that can be seen in 'processes, attitudes and behaviour which amount to discrimination through unwitting prejudice, ignorance, thoughtlessness and racist stereotyping' (para. 6.43).

The mental health professions have a history of various kinds of institutional racism. Our professional ancestors were central in constructing the idea of racial difference (see Chapter 2). We racialised schizophrenia. Black psychiatrists such as Suman Fernando (1991) began writing two decades ago about the many ways in which psychiatric services fail black and ethnic minority patients, and are still doing so (Fernando, 2010).

The counselling and psychotherapy profession was prompted to examine its practice. Currently, we too tend to fail racially marginalised people who use our services, as well as those who find our services too difficult or off-putting to access. We also fail to be professions in which racially marginalised clinicians and trainees feel welcome and adequately supported (McKenzie-Mavinga, 2016). These failings are institutional. They are not the fault of individual practitioners, but it is our collective responsibility to notice what needs to change – and to change it.

The Civil Rights activist Stokely Carmichael (Carmichael and Hamilton, 1969) was the first to use the term 'institutional racism', and he meant something different, though related, to the institutional racism that Macpherson defines. Today, we might use the term 'systemic racism' instead when referring to the larger system in which institutions such as the police play a role. Public institutions such as the police – and the mental health professions – operate within larger systems of ideals and ideas. Marx used the concept of 'ideology' with which to think about these systems: capitalism is an ideology, as is patriarchy and white supremacy.

Many of the movements referred to in Chapter 3 were concerned with ideology, and so clients who became politically aware in the 1970s and 1980s may think in terms of ideology. So might you if you are of a certain age, in which case it may be important to know that many contemporary movements, particularly Queer politics, are influenced by a very different understanding of power. Foucault's concept of 'discourse' is concerned with how we are controlled by ideas, and how these ideas (e.g. sexuality, 'race' or gender) are constructed.

Following on from the idea that one can understand how something works by taking it apart, 'deconstruction' involves understanding how these ideas are constructed. Being ideas, they are primarily constructed by language. Language matters. Language is power. Clients whose politics are influenced by Foucauldian thought are likely to be particularly sensitised to language as a means of power. 'Misgendering', for instance, is the term used by the trans community for using language that does not correspond to someone's gender identity. Misgendering is understood (and felt) as an act of violence.

There are important differences between the concepts of ideology and discourse, but, for the purposes of this chapter, what matters is an understanding that power operates in ways that are so embedded, so normal, so 'just how things are' that they can be difficult to recognise.

'We're all just people'

Recognising ideologies or discourses that perpetuate unjust social power relations is important in itself, both in the wider world and in the therapy room. The term 'colour-blindness' (in the political sense) originates with United States Supreme Court Justice John Marshal Harlan, who, in 1886 called for a colour-blind society, in which 'race' does not impact how one is treated (Smith, 2015). This society is yet to emerge, and so race does still matter. We are indeed all people – people who are either disadvantaged or advantaged by racism. We ignore this at our clients' peril. Being colour-blind is quite different to being anti-racist, which involves actively acknowledging and undermining racism.

The term 'difference-blindness' widens the concept of colour-blindness to include other 'differences' through which people are marginalised. Difference-blindness involves not a refusal to acknowledge overt acts of hostility, but a failure to recognise that we all live within ideologies and discourses that privilege some people at the expense of others.

Difference-blindness is not helpful to the young lawyer who feels pressurised to stay late at the office with a male colleague because it prevents her male therapist from understanding that she feels vulnerable. It prevents the working-class student's therapist from understanding how different she feels because she does not have access to the same economic, social and cultural capital as her friends. Difference-blindness prevents us from seeing how 'other' lives differ from our own. It limits one's ability to understand a client's context. It limits our capacity to empathise with any accuracy. We need to see the reality of clients' lives if we are to offer any real help.

The charmed circle

Being difference-blind is a denial of the reality that all lives are, in very different ways, impacted by inequality and by the systems, ideologies and discourses that sustain this inequality. It is particularly difficult to recognise this from a socially powerful position. To be part of a socially powerful group, part of the mainstream, is to live in a charmed circle in which legal, educational, economic and other social systems generally work in your favour and your group's norms are taken as the standard from which others differ.

The charmed circle is often invisible to those inside it, as is the reality of life outside the circle. Recognising and acknowledging the privileges we have as members of socially advantaged groups helps us to see the systems of privilege and disadvantage in which we – and our clients – live. This is vital if we are to understand anything about our marginalised client's life-experience – or how they attribute meaning to their experience.

In 1988, Peggy Mackintosh published a paper on unpacking the metaphorical knapsack of unearned privileges that she is given simply because she is white. These unearned privileges constitute an invisible and weightless knapsack (backpack) of maps, passports, visas, clothes, tools, and blank cheques that ease her passage through life. They include knowing that her race will not count against her if she needs medical or legal help, being (mostly) able to protect her children from people who may not like them, seeing people of her own colour represent her national heritage and being reasonably confident of finding a publisher for her article.

Thirty years later the idea of unearned privileges is finally becoming part of the public discussion of racism and some other systems of inequality. It is an important idea because it highlights that institutional and systemic discrimination remains a problem – and requires institutional and systemic change. In therapy, the more immediate point of recognising one's privileges is to use this awareness to avoid making unwarranted assumptions about othered clients and to understand that their social context is quite different to your own. In the longer term, the point, from a social justice perspective, of becoming aware of our unearned privileges is to use them to help dismantle the systems, ideologies and discourses that produce them and that cause or exacerbate our clients' suffering.

Reflective exercise

Bring to mind several clients (real or imagined) with marginalised identities in relation to your mainstream identities, e.g. if you are cisgendered, a trans client; or a working-class client if you are middle class, etc. Try to identify and list some of the privileges and opportunities you enjoy that your othered clients are denied. You might, for example, include privileges such as:

- feeling welcome in public places such as 'high-end' shops
- the police assuming that you are law-abiding
- being able to get into any building you might want to go to – and be able to find an accessible toilet while you're there
- feeling confident that strangers you come into contact with during the course of your daily life will not be insulting or aggressive towards you

Had you unconsciously assumed that all your clients also enjoy these privileges?
Spend some time thinking, writing or talking about how your client's life might have been impacted if they enjoyed the unearned privileges that ease your own life.

My white privilege has been engaged in the process of writing this book, which I am aware sounds angry at points. Had I been a black woman, I think I would have worried about engaging my reader's 'angry black woman' stereotype and what I have to say being dismissed on that basis. My privilege lies in not having to even think about the possibility that my anger might be discounted because of my race. Acknowledging that one's own life is made easier by the systemic oppression of others can be challenging, so challenging that the anti-racist trainer Robin DiAngelo (2018) uses the term 'white fragility' to describe a psychological state in which even a minimum amount of racial stress triggers a defensive reaction in white people.

This creates a climate in which any invitation to acknowledge racism causes more outrage among white people than the racism itself. Although there seems to be a particular sensitivity to being thought of as racist, calling out any kind of prejudice may elicit a defensive response. Being overtly defensive with a client who challenges you on a prejudice, or who brings up a subject – such as racism or sexism – that makes you uncomfortable, is clearly likely to damage the therapeutic relationship and be anti-therapeutic. Covertly defensive strategies such as avoiding difficult conversations, or closing down emotionally, are also therapeutically destructive.

White and 'majority' racial identity models

The identity models discussed in this section may be useful in assessing your fragility and your current suitability for working with clients from particular social groups. It begins by looking at Janet Helms's (1984) White Racial Identity Model, which grew out of her work with William Cross on black racial identity models. Helms is (obviously) thinking about 'race' but her model can also be used to think about other kinds of privileged identities. Ruth Hardiman and Bailey Jackson's (1997) Social Identity Development Model, discussed later in the section, does not focus on racism, but provides a general model of oppressive social relationships. Both models can be useful in reflecting upon therapeutic relationships in which there is a discrepancy in social power.

Racially marginalised people generally have no difficulty in identifying what their race means and how it impacts their lives. White people tend to find the question difficult to understand. The construction of a racial 'them' and 'us' has, because it was dreamt up and executed by white people, rendered whiteness the invisible norm against which people of colour stand out. This is one of the many ways in which white lives are also shaped by racism.

Helms (1984) sees the development of white identity as closely related to the development of racism, and argues that it is difficult to develop a positive white identity while denying the reality of racism. White people, she says, must make a conscious effort to understand how racism works to their advantage and make a deliberate effort to abandon it in favour of a non-racist white identity.

The assumptions underpinning Helms's (1984) White Racial Identity Theory are that white people are socialised to feel superior just because they are white (and may be under considerable social pressure to adopt racist attitudes), and secondly, that because they are not hurt by it, white people don't feel or notice racism. Hence they can easily avoid being aware of the ways in which they are socially advantaged at the expense of others. The same might be said of those racially privileged in other contexts: the Chinese in Singapore, for example, who are privileged in relation to the Malaysians, who in turn are privileged in relation to the Indians.

The model was revised in Helms (1995) and has two phases. The first phase consists of three statuses – Contact, Disintegration and Reintegration – which are concerned with the person's relationship with racism. The second, which also consists of three statuses – Pseudo-independence, Immersion–Emersion and Autonomy – describes the eventual formation of a non-racist white identity. As discussed in Chapter 3, Helms's statuses are dynamic. One may move between statuses or experience/exhibit the characteristic of more than one status at a time.

Helms's white identity statuses

Contact: 'I don't see race. Everyone is equal'

People in this status may consider themselves to be colour-blind and free of prejudice. They do not understand racism as a social system and are unaware of their own racism.

This status is characterised by a lack of awareness as to how racism creates inequalities and a denial of the impact of racism on one's own racially privileged life and on the life of the racially marginalised. One feels no responsibility for one's part in a dehumanising system.

A therapist in this status is likely to be oblivious to the relevance of race to their clients, themselves and to the therapeutic relationship.

Disintegration: 'This all feels very difficult and confusing. I don't like thinking about it'

One may move to this status as a result of witnessing racism or having interracial interactions that provoke awareness. One begins to see the workings of racism and experiences internal conflict, denying racism while witnessing it. One may experience intense feelings of guilt, helplessness, shame and anxiety, perhaps trying to reduce the emotional and cognitive confusion and conflict by avoiding racially marginalised people. People in this status may continue to deny the reality of racism – or start challenging racism.

A therapist with high Disintegration attitudes may feel anxious with a racially marginalised client, want their client to educate them about racism, or dismiss the real impact of racism and see the client as 'playing the race card'.

Reintegration: 'That's not racism – it's just common sense'

One way of resolving the conflict of the Disintegration status is to adopt explicitly racist attitudes. People in this status see racial privileges not as a product of racial inequality, but as earned, or even as their natural right. This status is a regressive step back towards racism.

A white therapist with high Reintegration attitudes is likely to be unaware of their fear and anger, and likely to be highly defensive in relation to race. They would need to work through all of this before it would be appropriate for them to work with racially marginalised clients.

Pseudo-independence: 'I'm not racist! ... (but I think you are!)'

One may enter this status if jolted from Reintegration by a painful or insightful encounter or event. Someone in this status begins to re-examine their beliefs about race and racism; they may become uncomfortable with being white and identify less and less with the prevailing racist climate. The Pseudo-independent status is characterised by a sense of not belonging that may be resolved by challenging racism – or colluding with it more closely.

This status is called 'Pseudo-independence' because someone in this status may seem free from racist ideology/discourse, but their understanding of race and racism is about externals – they have yet to examine themselves and their own lives.

A therapist in Pseudo-independence is likely to feel insecure in the presence of a racially marginalised client. They may have a genuine interest in working with marginalised clients, but lack any real understanding of the impact of racism.

Immersion–Emersion

Someone in this status starts to examine how they personally benefit from racism. When in Immersion–Emersion, one is likely to be more open to self-examination and may experience feelings that were previously outside awareness. One becomes increasingly willing to honestly confront one's own biases and to become more active in directly combating racism. There is an experiential and emotional understanding that was lacking in Pseudo-independence.

A therapist in Immersion–Emersion will be aware that they are at an early stage of self-awareness and although they may feel challenged by doing so, they are no longer so afraid of working with a marginalised client.

Autonomy

An increasing awareness of racial privilege, and acceptance of one's own role in perpetuating or challenging racism leads to Autonomy.

A therapist with high Autonomy attitudes is knowledgeable about diversity, and values it. They no longer feel anxious, fearful, embarrassed or defensive in discussing 'race' and racism, and are able to non-defensively facilitate a client in developing a positive racial identity.

> **Reflective exercise for racially privileged readers**
>
> Which of the above statuses (or aspects of them) do you recognise or identify with? Discuss the implications for your practice with your supervisor.

Helms (1984) uses this model to describe four types of cross-racial relationships: parallel, crossed, progressive and regressive:

The parallel relationship: therapist and client share similar attitudes towards 'race' and racialised groups.

The crossed relationship: therapist and client have different and opposing attitudes towards 'race' and racialised groups.

The progressive relationship: the therapist holds racial attitudes that are at a higher stage of identity development than the client and is therefore potentially able to facilitate the client's racial identity development.

The regressive relationship: the therapist is at a lower stage of racial identity development than the client and their understanding therefore severely limited. The client may well end the relationship.

> **Reflective exercise**
>
> Bring to mind a client whose social position in relation to 'race' – and/or class, gender, etc. – is less privileged than your own.
> Use Helms's relationship typology to think, write or talk about how your respective social positions impact the therapeutic relationship.

Helms's model has been adapted to develop identity development models for members of other majority groups. Jane Simoni and Karina Walters (2001), for instance, use Helms's five stages in their model of heterosexual identity development. Hardiman and Jackson's (1997) Social Identity Development Model addresses any mainstream or marginalised-identity development. A Transactional Analysis interpretation of their model is particularly memorable (although, regretfully, I cannot find its origin):

Reflective exercise

Depending on whether you are working alone or with others, think, write or talk about:

- which groups of people do you feel uncomfortable with. How might your attitude manifest in working with a client from that group?
- whether you feel awkward about your membership of a particular social group. How might this manifest in working with a client from a more or a less privileged group?

Hardiman and Jackson's model acknowledges that members of both mainstream and marginalised groups may actively or passively accept or reject oppressive discourses.

Case study

Sue, a therapist working in Further Education, actively joined in conversations with other staff about the students being unmotivated, lazy and work-shy. Isobel, her colleague, listened passively, silently agreeing. Tina, a student, had been referred to Sue. She admired Sue, whom she thought of as very kind. She looked up to her while Sue looked down on her. Tina thought of herself as thick and tried to learn from the inspirational quotes on Sue's counselling room wall.

After the fire at Grenfell Tower took so many lives, Sue felt sad about the deaths, especially the innocent children. However, both Tina and Isobel felt angry and their anger increased as it became evident that the fire had spread so quickly because the Tower was encased in combustible cladding. Sue listened patiently as Tina cried and raged in their next session. She wished Tina would stop talking about external events and get back on track by looking at their plan to improve her poor attendance at college. As the weeks progressed, Tina became increasingly irritated with Sue's smarmy smile and patronising tone. She stopped keeping her appointments and soon received an email telling her that she was no longer a client of the service.

Meanwhile, Isobel's understanding of the world was changing as she read about the lack of safety standards in social housing, and the disregard for those left bereaved, traumatised and without their homes and belongings. She developed a distaste for the reality television programmes such as *Benefits Street* that she had previously watched uncritically and started reading about the effects of austerity and the introduction of Universal Credit.

When Tina realised that the building that she lived in was covered in the same cladding as Grenfell Tower and that she and the other tenants were

(Continued)

expected to pay for its replacement, she re-referred herself to the service and asked to see another therapist. As you probably guessed, she was allocated to Isobel. When they began working together, Tina looked up to Isobel, as she had with Sue, seeing her as someone who would motivate her to get a great job and get out of her tower block. Tina's acceptance of the idea that she just needed to try harder began to rub against her increasing understanding of how the odds were stacked against her. She began to take an interest in community politics and joined a local pressure group. Isobel, who had been in active Resistance for some time, was delighted.

However, Isobel, who lived in a very well-heeled part of London, was also secretly terrified of Tina's anger at 'posh people who don't know and don't care about people like me'. She took her fear to supervision and worked hard over a number of extra sessions on how she saw herself in relation to the injustices around her. She emerged into Redefinition with the realisation that she too could become active in pressing for better health and safety standards in social housing. Unfortunately, she became so carried away that she found herself saying that Tina's pressure group should focus their energies in a slightly different way. Tina erupted with fury. She accused Isobel, and people like her, of being out of touch but trying to take over anyway. When she stormed out at the end of the session, Isobel was not sure if she would come back.

Isobel booked another extra supervision session. Her supervisor helped her to think about why she had become so invested in Tina's life, and also helped her to see how class politics were being played out in her relationship with Tina when she assumed a position of superior understanding and authority. She emerged chastened and when, to her relief, Tina appeared for their next session, she apologised for her arrogance. In the weeks that followed, she worked hard in supervision and personal therapy to integrate her growing political awareness. She only just kept up with Tina, who was doing the same in her sessions with Isobel. They were able to fruitfully repair the disruption to their relationship caused by Isobel's arrogance and went on to do some good work.

A few weeks before they ended, Isobel noticed that the door to Sue's office was wide open. Sue was not there, but her motivational quotations were. Tina now knew that the chances of her getting a great job or of getting out of her tower block were slim. She knew that she could not afford to pay for university fees on top of her living expenses, even with a loan and a couple of jobs. She had discovered that even professional jobs do not always pay so well – if at all in the beginning. She could not afford to be an intern. And she knew that she would be very unlikely ever to live in the dream house that she had imagined in so much detail. She was not in control of her life in the way that Sue had so often claimed, but she now knew that she had a choice in how to respond to the multiple ways in which she and 'other' people are maltreated.

Conclusion

Helms's White Racial Identity Theory and other early models trace the psychological process of developing an anti-racist identity, and it now looks as though 'white racial identity' was an unfortunate misnomer. Various scholars noted that these models looked at how white people feel about those who are racially othered, specifically African Americans, rather than at how they feel about being white, and how they might come to have a positive identity as white. This change in emphasis is in line with a tendency in American academia and public discourse to use a multicultural rather than an anti-discriminatory lens (see Chapter 5 for the difference between the two). Whiteness is not a cultural identity – being Belgian, or Basque, is a cultural identity. Whiteness only exists in the context of a racial hierarchy that was invented to benefit some at the expense of others.

This move towards understanding whiteness as a 'cultural identity' rather than as a function of social stratification has recently been echoed in populist political discourse. Ashley Jardina (2019) found that 30–40 per cent of white Americans say that a white identity is important to them. Jardina makes a distinction between those of her research subjects who held overtly racist views and those who have no particular antipathy towards other 'races', but want white people to retain privileges. It might be useful to understand those who are overtly racist as being, in Hardiman and Jackson's terms, in active Acceptance, and those seeking to protect privileges that they feel they are losing as being in passive Acceptance. Similar attitudes can be seen in Britain. The far right is working hard to normalise overtly racist attitudes while many others, who do not hold these attitudes, believe that they are somehow losing out to 'migrants'. The identity models discussed in this chapter are intended to help us recognise our privileges and the systems that confer them at the expense of the 'other'.

Understanding that rather than losing out to the 'other', we benefit from the ways in which 'they' lose out, can be a challenging process, but it is not optional if we are to offer othered clients the same quality of service that we offer to everybody else.

Further reading

European American Collaborative Challenging Whiteness Independent Scholar without Institutional Affiliation (2007) *Towards a Reexamination of White Identity Models*. Available at: www.iconoclastic.net/eccw/papers/eccw2007c.pdf (accessed 12 September 2019).

Helms, J. (2017) 'The challenge of making whiteness visible: Reactions to four whiteness articles', *The Counseling Psychologist*, 45(5): 717–26.

Lensmire, T.J., McManimon, S.K., Tierney, J.D., Lee-Nichols, M.E., Casey, Z.A., Lensmire, A. and Davis, B.M. (2013) 'McIntosh as synecdoche: How teacher education's focus on white privilege undermines antiracism', *Harvard Educational Review*, 83(3): 410–31.

Tuckwell, G. (2002) *Racial Identity, White Counsellors and Therapists*. Buckingham: Open University Press.

Wijeyesinghe, C.L and Jackson, B.W. III (2001) *New Perspectives on Racial Identity Development: A Theoretical and Practical Anthology*. New York: New York University Press.

11
Challenges to Communication

'Did you get my message?'

Learning aims

- To appreciate the importance of using language that does not jar with the client.
- To consider whether and how the language codes identified by Basil Bernstein and the gendered process of framing identified by Deborah Tannen might impact the therapeutic relationship.
- To think about issues that might arise when either the client or the therapist is working in an additional language.
- To understand what good practice in working with interpreters looks like.

Language is the central medium through which therapy is conducted – even art therapy and body psychotherapy. Language is also a central medium through which 'difference' and inequality are created and sustained. As Chapters 2 and 3 demonstrate, social stratification is, in part, construed through ideas, i.e. language. Clearly, it is important to try to use language in a way that avoids replicating a hostile social relationship. This chapter begins by discussing language that a client might find wounding. It goes on to discuss more subtle ways in which social identities impact the way we speak, and what we hear. It then identifies issues that might arise when either therapist or client is working in an additional language and ends with an in-depth look at best practice when working with an interpreter.

Mind your language

One of the risks in working with those who have been othered is that they are alienated or hurt by the language that you use. Racist, sexist, homophobic and other hateful terms are powerful because of their contribution to the social imagery that has helped create and sustain unequal social relationships. The implication of words – particularly the words used to identify the 'other' – changes over time. Few of the terms acceptable a few decades ago are still acceptable today, and some of the terms used in this book will also become dated. Language becomes associated with the attitudes of particular eras, which is one of the reasons why the term 'coloured', popular in the 1950s and 1960s, is offensive to many, while the current term 'people of colour' is not. 'People of colour' is a term chosen by racially marginalised people (Ross, 2011) rather than a pejorative term that has been imposed. However, not all people of colour like the term (Shoneye, 2018). Its most appropriate use is in pointing to a common experience of racism. Otherwise, it is usually more appropriate to distinguish between different groups rather than lumping them together as 'not white'. If you're not sure how your client identifies, ask them (preferably when it is relevant to the conversation). The racial identity models discussed in Chapters 3 and 4 may be helpful if you sense that you don't quite understand what your client's chosen term means to them. It may be important to keep in mind that your client may identify as, for instance, black in one context, as African Caribbean in another and as Jamaican in another.

Trans clients are likely to particularly appreciate care when it comes to the way in which you use language. A trans client may indicate their preferred pronouns in their initial email (if this is how they first make contact). You are, of course, unlikely to refer to them in the third person when speaking to them, but the way in which you refer to them when speaking about them (in supervision, obviously) also matters. There is more about contemporary gender terminology in Chapter 4.

There are a number of abusive terms that marginalised groups have reclaimed and use with pride ('dyke', 'queer', etc.). Using these terms if you are not a member of that group can be a delicate negotiation, and best avoided unless you are very familiar and comfortable with that community – and have been accepted as an ally. Even then, it is still necessary to communicate your ally-ship to your client. A client I was seeing for the first time just would not stop talking at the end of the session, introducing one new issue after another. I picked up my diary, put on my glasses, and said, several times, that we needed to finish while he talked over me. Then I had a sudden intuition that he was waiting for a fuller response to his having come out earlier. I re-engaged with the conversation, taking it back to the subject of his sexual identity and made a very 'in' joke. As he elaborated upon the joke in response, he stood up and put his coat on. I had told him what he had been waiting to hear.

Speaking in code

One of Anne Kearney's (Kearney, 2018) central arguments in *Counselling, Class and Politics* is predicated upon the educationalist Basil Bernstein's theory of language codes. Bernstein (1964) wanted to account for the relatively poor performance of working-class pupils in language-based subjects, while otherwise doing as well as their middle-class counterparts in other subjects. He proposed that while middle-class children have access to both an 'elaborated' and a 'restricted' language code, working-class children only have access to a restricted code. Elaborated code is a way of speaking that is detailed and specific, e.g. 'my husband, George McFee, the architect' – the speaker elaborates on what they say in order to make their meaning clear. Restricted code is stripped of detail and relies heavily on implication and shared understanding. An anonymous 'him' or 'he' is an example of restricted code that assumes that the listener will understand that the man referred to is the speaker's husband. Somebody using elaborated code would be likely to specify that 'he' is her (or his) husband, and perhaps also reveal his name. A middle-class client who simply refers to him by name, leaving you to work out that 'Peter' is her husband is using restricted code in a characteristically middle-class way.

Kearney mentions controversial ideas about how using different codes impacts the ways in which we think, only to say that she is not concerned with those ideas, but with the social power (or lack of it) associated with each code (one might think, Bourdieu's terms, of elaborated code as having much more cultural capital than restricted code).

The dangers that Kearney identifies include missing the emotional significance of what a client says – or underestimating the sophistication of their understanding – because restricted code has less social value and we therefore unwittingly devalue what is said because of the way in which it is said, thus exacerbating the power imbalance within the therapeutic relationship. Clients using restricted code assume that you understand what they mean. It can be difficult to spot when you don't. The temptation is to fill in the gaps of meaning from one's own class-based perspective, again exacerbating the power imbalance.

Kearney acknowledges the difficulty of facilitating an exploration of emotional experience when a client's vocabulary is limited. However, when writing about how class and language impact the therapeutic relationship, Bernstein's (1964) focus is not upon a limited vocabulary, but upon a different vocabulary. He understands therapy's focus upon the articulation of personal, emotional experience as instrumental in creating an inhospitable environment for working-class clients. Bernstein argues that restricted code, with its assumption of shared meanings, is geared towards articulating similarity and social identity, not the articulation of particularity and personal identity with which therapy is concerned. Those who can only access restricted code, he observes, express their personal as opposed to their social selves nonverbally. We can make use of this observation to listen much harder to what is said without words.

Case study

'Well, that's him away.'

'Who?'

'My old dad'

'Away where?'

'Gone.'

'What? ... Your dad's died? ... he has? ... Oh, my goodness. Oh my goodness. Just give me a moment to let that sink in.'

My client nods, says, 'yes, I know.' She was close to her father, but says nothing of how she feels. Instead she tells me about the funeral arrangements in great detail. I hear the care she is putting into getting everything just right, a good send-off. She pauses. She looks crumpled. I give her a 'this is so sad' look. She returns my look. She sighs. She looks at the floor. We sit in silence for a while. There is no need for words.

Frames and filters

Deborah Tannen (1991) uses the idea that women and men 'frame' language differently. Men, she argues, understand what is said through a hierarchical filter, whereas women understand what is said from a perspective of an equal and cooperative relationship. Thus a woman is likely to understand your enquiry as to how you can help as motivated by your desire to help another person on an interdependent web of relationships, whereas a man might well hear it as an attempt to push him down the relationship hierarchy. I find the idea that we can frame what is said from a hierarchical or a flat perspective more useful than the idea that this is necessarily determined by gender. I, for instance, found the idea of framing in terms of hierarchies very helpful in understanding a particular client's defensiveness. Her hierarchical framing stemmed from the culture in her profession, not her gender.

Reflective exercise

Depending on whether you are working alone or with others, think, write or talk about instances from your own practice, or your own life, that affirm the idea that men and women interpret what they hear differently. What were the particular

> circumstances? Who was interacting, and in what context? Do you think that the particular circumstances or context had a bearing on the interpretation made? Can you think of instances that challenge the idea that communication is gendered in such a straightforward way?

The cross-cultural counselling literature that attributes particular characteristics to large groups of people, such as 'Asians', tends to also claim that these monolithic groups have characteristic ways of communicating. This is simplified knowledge (as defined in Chapter 5). There is usually some truth in simplified knowledge, but the context really does make all the difference. A casual flick through some of the literature on cross-cultural communication tells me that, in China, it is not considered appropriate for someone with less authority to maintain eye contact with a person who has more. Doing so is considered challenging and disrespectful. I should not interpret a Chinese client who avoids eye contact as being defensive.

I've not been to China, but I have taught many Chinese students who have come to Scotland to study, and so know that I need to take care in using this kind of information. Most of the Chinese students that I teach maintain eye contact with me when we speak. Were I to take the simplified knowledge at face value, I would have to believe that these students are being disrespectful. Everything about their manner tells me otherwise. It may well be that my students maintain eye contact with me in a way that they would not with a lecturer who was Chinese. My assumption is that they are adept at processing social information with regard to its context.

I also have experience of being stared at, by both Chinese and European students, in a manner that very much felt like a challenge to my authority. This felt very different to the way in which students normally hold my gaze as we speak. Most therapists – and most clients – are highly sensitised to the 'feel' of an interaction. We should not disregard this as a source of information. The best use of any preconceived, simplified knowledge is to hold it in mind as a possibility, but to otherwise rely upon the sophisticated manner with which we all normally interpret social information in its context. If a therapeutic relationship or interaction does not feel right, it is appropriate to explore whether there may be some intercultural miscommunication happening.

Working in an additional language

Sometimes therapy is conducted in a language that is an additional language for either the client or the therapist (or both). This may happen for all manner of reasons, one of the most common reasons being that either the client or the therapist (or both) is an international student.

Research shows that, unsurprisingly, trainees beginning their practice in a language that they are (to varying degrees) still learning feel anxious about being seen as incompetent. One of the interviewees in Lorena Georgiadou's (2015) research makes the interesting observation that this could be as much to do with being a novice therapist as to do with working in an additional language. However, trainees who are not confident in their language skills, and who, on top of everything else, may have to make out a client's accent or dialect, will have to work harder. If you are working in an additional language, it may be important to account for therapeutic work taking more energy than it does for your native-speaking peers. Georgiadou (2015) offers encouragement by also finding positive aspects to working in an additional language, including more opportunities for the client to clarify their meaning.

Clients may be working in an additional language because they do not have the choice of working in their first language, or because doing so is not a priority. Either way there are some considerations to hold in mind. Binyavanga Wainaina, whose memoir was recommended in Chapter 7, writes about how, in Kenya, people switch languages depending on whether they want to invite a more intimate or a more formal relationship, or something in between. He also observes that, conversely, switching language changes the interaction. Being the language associated with colonialism, English, as you might guess, is used for/gives rise to more distant relationships. What speaking English means to any particular client will, of course, vary. Several Anglo-Indian clients that I worked with understood it as a bond between us, an expression of shared culture rather than as the language of the coloniser and colonised.

Making a distinction between working in a client's second (or third or fourth) language and not working in their first language helps highlight what they might lose (and gain) from not using their mother tongue. There may be concepts in the client's first language that do not have an easy linguistic equivalent in English, such as the Filipino *tampo*, which means withdrawing affection from a person who has hurt one's feelings or the Czech word *litost*, which describes an emotional experience that blends grief, sympathy, remorse and longing.

The experience, as opposed to the practical challenges, of not speaking their first language may have an impact on the client's process. As one of the participants in Efrosini Kokaliari et al.'s (2013) research says, the emotionally laden meaning of the words one grew up with are inevitably a little thinner in meaning when translated into another language. Language and memory and emotional experience are very much intertwined. Kokaliari et al. found that bilingual clients tend to use their first language for emphasis or to express nuances in feeling, with one research participant noticing that her clients' language becomes more sensory when speaking in their mother tongue.

Several of the research participants said that their clients tended to use their first language when describing traumatic experiences, particularly if the trauma happened when they were very young. Some encouraged this in the interests of the client making good contact with their emotional experience, even if it meant that the therapist did not understand what the client was saying. This, as the authors point out, risks the therapist not understanding an overwhelmed client. There are no clear rules, but rather a judgment call on the balance of risk and benefit.

A plan is in order if one does decide to take a risk. Were I a therapist whose client had become overwhelmed in a language I do not speak or understand, I would use the language that we do share to make present-day contact with them. In doing so, I would be doing exactly what I would do with any other overwhelmed or dissociated client. The therapists participating in Kokaliari et al.'s research also talked about how a second language can create distance from traumatic material. Some framed this in terms of repression, and some as creating a safe distance.

What it means when a traumatised client chooses to use or avoid their mother tongue very much depends on the specific context. It is important to be aware of the potential advantages and risks in order to work with your client's choice in an informed and safe manner. A couple of Kokaliari et al.'s participants noted that trauma can be more difficult to talk about in a first language if that language does not recognise the events being referred to as traumatic (it is, for example, only quite recently that 'childhood sexual abuse' has come to replace the earlier 'incest' in English). It may not only be trauma that can be difficult to talk about in one's mother tongue. I have had several clients for whom English was an additional language tell me that they find it easier to discuss their emotional life in English because they had not, while growing up, been encouraged to speak about how they felt. They had not really found the words for how they felt until having therapy, and as we were doing therapy in English, they'd become more able to talk about their emotional life in English.

The kinds of issues (if any) that arise when working in a client's additional language obviously vary depending on their language skills. It may be appropriate to make sure that you are not speaking too quickly, and to avoid using colloquialisms. Your client may find using English very tiring – and, especially if they have a strong accent and/or a limited vocabulary, you may also tire more quickly. You may want to consider this when planning your diary or, if you are not in control of your diary, to find some way of replenishing yourself quickly.

Two first-hand accounts of learning an additional language may be helpful in developing empathy for those clients who are still learning the language that you are working in. Katherine Russell Rich's (2011) *Dreaming in Hindi: Life in Translation* is concerned with a basic struggle to understand and make herself understood. Jhumpa Lahiri (2015) whose mother tongue is Bengali and who has written a number of (very good) novels in English, has fallen so deeply in love with Italian that she has decided that this will be the language she writes in, and so her account (which is written in both Italian and English) is more joyous.

Working with an interpreter

Working with an interpreter may be preferable, or necessary, for some clients. Given all the reasons as to why a client's relative or friend would not normally sit in on a session, it is clearly inappropriate for a client's relative or friend, rather than a professional, to interpret for therapy. Nor should the communicator who supports a d/Deaf client be used as an interpreter in therapy (see Chapter 3 for an explanation of 'd/Deaf'). If you are on placement or employed, it is likely that your agency already has an interpretation service that they use, or will do the work of finding a suitable interpreter should you need one. If you are seeing a client through an organisation, the organisation should pay the interpreter's fee.

If you need to find an interpreter yourself, Jude Boyles and Nathalie Talbot's (2017) *Working with Interpreters in Psychological Therapy* provides a detailed guide to finding the right interpreter. When working with a d/Deaf client, BACP recommends using an interpreter who is registered with a regulatory body such as the National Register of Public Service Interpreters, the National Register of Communication Professionals working with Deaf and Deafblind People or the Chartered Institute of Linguists (CIOL). Private practitioners who work with interpreters should have a clear agreement with the client about who books the interpreter and pays their fee.

You are ultimately responsible for ensuring the integrity and safety of the therapeutic space so, however you come by an interpreter, you should double-check the following:

- That the interpreter is qualified and working to a code of ethics.
- That the same interpreter is able to commit for the duration of the therapy.
- That you have accessed an interpreter who can work in the required dialect. Some languages differ substantially depending on where they are spoken. Sign language also varies from country to country. British Sign Language (BSL), Irish Sign Language (ISL), Sign Supported English (SSE) and cued speech are all used in the UK (SSE involves signing spoken English words and cued speech gestures explain words that cannot be easily lip read). A deaf client from another country may need an interpreter fluent in their particular sign language.
- Few commentators think that working on the telephone, or online, is desirable when working with a translator, but sometimes there are good reasons for doing so. Remember that automated web or application-based translation technologies often translate literally and so may be inaccurate or fail to make enough sense. If you cannot use a human being to interpret at least make sure that the technology you use is good enough.

If possible you should use an interpreter that is not known to the client from other professional (or social) relationships. Let the client know in advance who the proposed interpreter is and invite questions (you will probably do this through whomever is making the referral). The client may know the interpreter and/or have worries about confidentiality if they are from the same small language community as the interpreter (this includes the Deaf community). If they are not from the same small language community, there may be historical or political hostility between the interpreter's and the client's communities that would potentially impact the work. Gender may be a consideration, or age. Only the client knows whom they feel safe working with. Agree a way in which the client can let you know, in the session, if they are not, after all, happy with the interpreter.

Before therapy begins

Once an interpreter has been chosen you should meet them in advance of meeting the client. Explaining your therapeutic model and what the session is likely to involve will help the interpreter translate what you say in a way that is meaningful to your client. Although an interpreter's role is to translate what is said, a literal interpretation may be inadequate, particularly when talking about emotional experience. The interpreter may need to take the client's social and cultural context into account in order to remain faithful to the nuances of what is said. They may also have to use more words and speak for longer than you did as they ensure that the client understands.

You may also want to check out how comfortable the interpreter is with self-injury, suicidal feelings, dissociation, regression, hallucinations, talking about sex, being gay or trans, crying, anger, swearing and blaspheming. Ask them not to interrupt silences. Ask them to translate everything, including any question that the client may ask them, and to not ask the client additional questions without checking whether this is okay with you. It will probably be easier for you if, rather than translating simultaneously, a spoken language interpreter translates every couple of sentences or so. This sequential interpreting is usual in spoken language interpreting, but not with sign language interpretation where it is more usual for the interpreter to sign as you speak.

It may help you establish a connection with the client if, when translating, the interpreter speaks in the first person, as if they were the client. Agree how the interpreter can let you know if they need you (or the client) to speak more slowly. Agree a way of addressing any misunderstanding. Boyles and Talbot (2017) suggest asking the interpreter to keep their mobile phone in silent mode and out of sight as clients who have been persecuted may wonder if it is being used to record them. Obviously, you should also keep your phone switched off and out of sight.

Discuss the possibility that the session may be unsettling or distressing. Explain that you have a supervisor to help you process what you hear and let the interpreter know that you have set aside some time for them to debrief with you after the session. Let the interpreter know that needing and using emotional support is okay and that they will not be negatively judged if they also need or use support. It may also be important to discuss how the interpreter can manage their own feelings in the moment without intruding upon the therapy.

Explain that the client is likely to seek a lot of eye contact with the interpreter at the beginning of the working relationship, and ask them to reduce the eye contact they give in response as the therapeutic relationship develops.

If the possibility of the interpreter and client meeting in another context has not already become part of the conversation, you should raise that possibility. Explain why having another kind of relationship with the client outside therapy is better avoided, and emphasise the importance of absolute confidentiality.

Agree whether the interpreter will introduce themselves and briefly summarise their code of ethics, or whether you will do this while they interpret. You should also let the interpreter know in advance that there will be an opportunity for everyone to say goodbye to each other when ending and that you will let them know in advance if you plan to invite them to say anything about what working with the client and being part of the therapy has meant to them.

It may be important to avoid arriving with the interpreter when you meet the client so as to not provoke any fantasy that the two of you are in an alliance that excludes the client. Nor should the client and interpreter be thrown together if they arrive early. This may mean inviting the interpreter to wait in an office rather than a waiting room.

Contracting with the client

Ensure that the client understands that both you and the interpreter will not discuss what they say with anyone else. Explain the legal exceptions to confidentiality, and any obligations you have to pass on information to someone else in your organisation. You should also explain what supervision is and how you will protect your client's anonymity in supervision. If you are going to give the interpreter a chance to debrief afterwards (more about this later), you should explain to the client that you will not be talking about them, but discussing how the process of translation is working.

Make it clear that the interpreter's role is solely to support communication between you and the client. Explain why the therapeutic relationship would be compromised if you were to have another relationship with them outside therapy, and that some of the same dangers apply to them having another kind of relationship with the interpreter outside therapy. Discuss the possibility of them unexpectedly seeing you or the interpreter in another context and agree how that should be managed.

Ask if the client has worked with an interpreter before, and if not, explain the necessity of allowing time for the interpreter to translate every couple of sentences or so. Make sure that everyone feels able to ask everyone else to slow down or to clarify what they have said.

The 2018 General Data Protection Regulation (GDPR) requires you to seek both the client's and interpreter's permission to store any information about them, including basic contact information. You need to let them know who will have access to the information, and how long you intend to keep it. Documents seeking the client's agreement and any other written information should be in whatever language the client requests (which may not be the same language that they are speaking with the interpreter). Sign languages do not have a written form and many Deaf clients do not read English and so you will have to come to a mutually agreeable way of recording their permission.

The session

There are a number of different seating arrangements that seem to work. Some triads sit in an equidistant triangle. Some therapists prefer the interpreter to sit behind the client so that they do not intrude upon the therapeutic dyad, although this does prevent the interpreter from seeing the client's expressions and gestures. Many sign language interpreters prefer to sit next to the therapist so that the client can easily see both. A sign language interpreter will probably want to avoid sitting in front of a window or light because it is harder for the client to see the interpreter's hands clearly if they are in shadow. Whatever arrangement you choose (and this will, in part, depend upon the size of the room), make sure that you and your client can see and address each other directly, and remember that the client may well attribute meaning to whomever sits closest to whom.

It is important that the therapeutic relationship remains central. Be ready to end the session if the client seems to be uncomfortable with the interpreter. Avoid having a conversation with the interpreter that excludes the client, and query any conversation that the client and interpreter are having that seems to exclude you. Speak directly to your client rather than asking the interpreter to tell them something or ask them a question. Ask the interpreter to translate anything that the client addresses to them. You are responsible for the therapeutic space, and it is appropriate to exert your authority in order to protect it. Explore any possible misunderstandings during the session.

In ordinary conversation, one tends to look at whoever is speaking, so you may need to make an effort to look at your client when the interpreter is speaking or signing – so long as your client seems comfortable with your gaze, of course. It is usually best to maintain eye contact with d/Deaf clients while speaking to them, and to speak only when signing has stopped. Boyles and Talbot (2017) suggest that when working on the telephone or online, that you say hello and goodbye to your client yourself, either in English or in the client's language. If you are working on the telephone or online, you should speak a little more slowly than normal (and make your nonverbal communications verbal, or visible). Otherwise, speak at your usual speed, unless the interpreter asks you to slow down. Use ordinary language rather than therapy jargon where you can. If you really have to use a special term, explain what you mean by it. Sign language interpreters may have to invent signs for special terms, and spoken language interpreters may have to explain them at some length.

After the session

Set aside some time to meet with the interpreter after the session. Exchange feedback on anything that was unclear or that caused concern. It can also be useful to ask for feedback on anything that was particularly helpful to the interpreter, and for you to tell them if they did anything you found particularly helpful. Check how well the interpreter understands your way of working and identify whether there is a need for further explanation or training. It is important also to check your own learning needs. The interpreter may be able to explain a cultural context or nuance that you did not understand.

BACP's Good Practice in Action Fact Sheet 091, *Working with Interpreters in the Counselling Professions* (Chaturvedi, 2018) gives the therapist responsibility for identifying and addressing any vicarious trauma suffered by the interpreter. Interpreters who work in languages associated with areas of conflict or political repression can hear a great number of disturbing accounts, and this makes them more vulnerable to vicarious trauma. Vicarious or secondary trauma arises from identification with the speaker's emotional experience and characteristically changes how safe the listener feels in the world. Splevins et al. (2010) suggest that the verbatim translation of a client's traumatic experiences increases interpreters' involvement in the story and triggers identification (and one might speculate that this likelihood is exacerbated if the interpreter is speaking in the first person). The interpreter may also have had their own traumatic experience, perhaps even of the same situation the client is speaking about. Some of their own memories and responses may become activated.

Clearly you should be on the lookout for both vicarious and reactivated trauma. Speaking with the same intensity as the client may indicate that the interpreter has over-identified. If they have dissociated, they will be unaware of having done so. Boyles and Talbot (2017) suggest that the interpreter using the same tense as the client may indicate dissociation. Debriefing, talking about how they have been impacted by the session, helps prevent vicarious trauma. You cannot be the interpreter's therapist, but if you think that they need further support you can – and should – recommend that their employers pay for appropriate support.

Three people in the therapy room is quite different from two, especially if the third person is another professional. You may want to use supervision to reflect on the power relationships in the room (and those that intrude from the outside). Are there any unspoken alliances? Do you feel excluded? Does the interpreter feel valued? Might the client feel isolated? The British Psychological Society (2017) suggests considering some sort of joint supervision for psychologists and interpreters. As therapists use (and are given) supervision in a variety of quite different ways, this may be something for some to consider, but not others.

Further reading

Working in a second language

Bowker, P. and Richards, B. (2004) 'Speaking the same language? A qualitative study of therapists' experiences of working in English with proficient bilingual clients', *Psychodynamic Practice*, 10(4): 459–78.

Dewaele, J.-M. and Costa, B. (2013) 'Multilingual clients' experience of psychotherapy', *Language and Psychoanalysis*, 2(2): 31–50.

Working with interpreters

Boyles, J. and Talbot, N. (2017) *Working with Interpreters in Psychological Therapy: The Right to be Understood*. London: Routledge.

Quinn, L. (2011) 'Working with interpreters in psychotherapy', *Contemporary Psychotherapy*, 3(1). Available at: www.contemporarypsychotherapy.org/vol-3-no1-spring-2011/working-with-interpreters-in-therapy/ (accessed 21 March 2019).

Tribe, R. and Thompson, K. (2009) 'Exploring the three way relationship in therapeutic work with interpreters', *International Journal of Migrant Health and Social Care*, 5(2): 13–21.

Conclusion: The Therapeutic Relationship

'We meet at last'

Is all the effort demanded by the preceding chapters really necessary? Research affirms that it is. Doris Chang and Alexandra Berk (2009), who researched clients' satisfaction with cross-racial therapy, found that clients who were unsatisfied experienced their therapist as lacking an understanding of racism. Some felt that their therapist was racially or ethnically biased and some described therapists 'gaslighting'. Clients reported being disappointed by their therapist's ignorance of racial/ethnic and multi-racial/ethnic identity development. They were also disappointed by their therapist's lack of cultural understanding and skill in communication. Some found their therapist's responses too 'textbook', one participant complaining that her therapist seemed to have an image of a typical immigrant family rather than any emotional understanding of her particular experience. Even clients who were satisfied with their cross-racial therapy had avoided talking about race-related issues for fear of alienating their white therapists.

Research into the impact of class on the therapeutic relationship also points to the necessity of therapists making an effort. Jane Balmforth (2009) confirms Joanna Ryan (2006) and Gillian Proctor's (2006) assertion that therapeutic progress is hindered when therapists ignore class-related issues. Balmforth found that clients experiencing class-related feelings of shame or inferiority felt unable to raise class as an issue with their therapist. Several of the clients that she interviewed felt that it was the therapist's responsibility to raise class as an issue.

Research into working with clients with other marginalised identities draws similar conclusions about the importance of:

- understanding how a client's life is impacted by inequality and social hostility
- understanding how particular clients relate to their marginalised identities
- the importance of recognising one's own cultural values and appreciating one's client's values
- examining one's own prejudices and privileges.

This book has discussed a number of ideas, models and pieces of guidance intended to facilitate these on-going tasks. It has also encouraged you to think critically about these resources and to think about how best to use them. Resources can be used well or badly.

Working with clients from marginalised groups can provoke anxiety. It can be tempting to allay this anxiety by reaching for guidance or tools. The risk is that we may use them in a way that actually impedes rather than nurtures an emotionally engaged relationship. If, for example, you explore the literature on minority identity development models further, you will find a number of tools with which to measure your client's identity development. Tools such as these risk objectifying the client. They risk oversimplification. They tempt us into telling, rather than hearing. Marginalised and mainstream identity development models are perhaps most useful when used to gauge whether a particular therapist and client are a good 'fit' for each other.

One of the most striking features of Chang and Beck's research is that although the participating clients were not questioned about relational factors, they gave huge importance to the quality of the therapeutic relationship. Most volunteered information on how engaged and attentive – or inattentive and disengaged – the therapist had been. Unsurprisingly, those who were satisfied with their therapy had experienced their therapist as emotionally engaged; those who were dissatisfied had not. Trott (2016), researching class differences in the therapeutic dyad, also found that clients valued the quality of the therapeutic relationship above all else. Writing about therapy with transgender clients, Bockting and colleagues (2006) point out that trust and authenticity is essential to any successful therapeutic relationship, and so bring us back to the contention made at the beginning of this book that clients with marginalised identities are not different kinds of beings who require something different to 'normal' clients.

The psychologist and blogger Monnica Williams (2014) makes a point of saying that she does not speak for all African Americans, but the research evidence suggests that, with a few tweaks, she might speak for all clients:

> I can't speak for all African Americans, but I can tell you what I want – an authentic connection. That means that I want you to understand my experience. I want you to ask hard questions and not judge me when I give you the hard truth. I want you to take the time and effort to see the world as I do. I want to be seen as a whole person and not a stereotype. I want you to know how being an American can be a source of pride and pain. I want you to understand the harm caused by discrimination

and join me in speaking out against injustice and inequality. I want you to embrace cultural differences rather than merely tolerate them. I want you to celebrate with me the strengths and beauty of my culture. I want you to cry with me when racism and hatred win. I want to be able to connect with you as someone who is both different and the same. I want you to understand that differences are what make us special and the similarities are what make us human.

References

Abdolah, K. (2010) *The House of the Mosque* (trans. Susan Massotty). Edinburgh: Canongate.
Abu-Lughod, L. (1991) 'Writing against culture', in R.G. Fox (ed.), *Recapturing Anthropology: Working in the Present*. Santa Fe, CA: School of American Research Press. pp. 137–62.
Addonia, S. (2018) *Silence is my Mother Tongue*. London: Indigo Press.
Adichie, C.N. (2006) *Half of a Yellow Sun*. New York: Alfred A. Knopf.
Akala (2018) *Natives: Race and Class in the Ruins of Empire*. London: Hodder & Stoughton.
Allport, G. (1954) *The Nature of Prejudice*. Boston, MA: Addison-Wesley.
Alston, P. (2019) *Visit to the United Kingdom of Great Britain and Northern Ireland: Report of the Special Rapporteur on Extreme Poverty and Human Rights*. Available at: https://digitallibrary.un.org/record/3806308 (accessed 17 August 2019).
Anti-Slavery (2019) *Slavery in the UK*. Available at: www.antislavery.org/slavery-today/slavery-uk/ (accessed 7 September 2019).
Aries, E. and Seider, M. (2007) 'The role of social class in the formation of identity: A study of public and elite private college students', *The Journal of Social Psychology*, 147(2): 137–57.
BACP (British Association for Counselling and Psychotherapy) (2013) *Therapy Today: The international issue*, 24(7).
Balmforth, J. (2009) 'The weight of class: Clients' experiences of how perceived differences in social class between counsellor and client affect the therapeutic relationship', *British Journal of Guidance & Counselling*, 37(3): 375–86.
Bassey, S. and Melluish, S. (2013) 'Cultural competency for mental health practitioners: A selective narrative review', *Counselling Psychology Quarterly*, 26(2): 151–73.
Berer, M. (2019) *How not to Succeed in Publishing a Paper on an FGM Trial, and Keep Trying*. Available at: https://bererblog.wordpress.com/?s=FGM (accessed 10 September 2019).
Bernstein, B. (1964) 'Social class, speech systems and psycho-therapy', *The British Journal of Sociology*, 15(1): 54–64.
Binkley, J. and Koslofsky, S. (2017) 'Una familia unida: Cultural adaptation of family-based therapy for bulimia with a depressed Latina adolescent', *Clinical Case Studies*, 16(1): 25–41.
Blackless, M., Chanuvastra, A., Derryck, A., Fasto-Sterling, A., Lausanne, K. and Lee, E. (2000) 'How sexually diamorphic are we? Review and synthesis', *American Journal of Human Biology*, 12(2): 151–66.
Blair, V. (2002) 'The malleability of automatic stereotypes and prejudice', *Personality and Social Psychology Review*, 6(3): 242–61.
Bliss, C. (2015) *Race Decoded: The Genomic Fight for Social Justice*. Stanford, CA: Stanford University Press.
Bloor, D. (1991) *Knowledge and Social Imagery*, 2nd edn. Chicago, IL: University of Chicago Press.
Blumenbach, J.F. (1865) *Anthropological Treatises of Blumenbach and Hunter*. London: Longman.

Bockting, W.O., Knudson, G. and Goldberg, J.M. (2006) 'Counseling and mental health care for transgender adults and loved ones', *International Journal of Transgenderism*, 9(3–4): 35–82.

Boochani, B. (2018) *No Friend but the Mountains: Writing from Manus Prison*. London: Picador.

Bourdieu, P. (1986) 'The forms of capital', in J. Richardson (ed.), *Handbook of Theory and Research for the Sociology of Education*. New York: Greenwood. pp. 241–58.

Boyles, J. and Talbot, N. (2017) *Working with Interpreters in Psychological Therapy: The Right to be Understood*. London: Routledge.

Branigan, T. (2014) 'It's good to talk: China opens up to psychotherapy', *The Guardian*, 3 September. Available at: www.theguardian.com/world/2014/sep/03/china-psychiatrists-talking-therapy-counselling (accessed 28 August 2019).

British Psychological Society (2017) *Working with Interpreters: Guidelines for Psychologists*. Leicester: BPS.

Bulman, M. (2019a) 'Home Office "illegally" put trafficking victims in detention centres, report finds', *The Independent*, 29 July. Available at: www.independent.co.uk/news/uk/home-news/home-office-modern-slavery-victims-trafficking-immigration-detention-labour-exploitation-advisory-a9019361.html (accessed 7 September 2019).

Bulman, M. (2019b) 'Trafficking victims "forced into homelessness and re-exploitation" as they are denied immigration status', *The Independent*, 30 July. Available from: www.independent.co.uk/news/uk/home-news/home-office-modern-slavery-victims-trafficking-immigration-detention-labour-exploitation-advisory-a9019361.html (accessed 7 September 2019).

Burns, L. (2018) *The Milkman*. London: Faber and Faber.

Butler, J. (1990) *Gender Trouble: Feminism and the Subversion of Identity*. New York: Routledge.

Butler, J. (1993) *Bodies That Matter: On the Discursive Limits of 'Sex'*. New York: Routledge.

Cameron, R. (2017) 'Politics, prejudice, power and privilege', in J. Tolan with R. Cameron, *Skills for Person Centred Counselling and Psychotherapy*, 3rd edn. London: Sage. pp. 125–38.

Carmichael, S. and Hamilton, C.V. (1969) *Black Power: The Politics of Liberation in America*. Harmondsworth: Penguin.

Carpenter, S. and Banaji, M.R. (2001) 'Malleability in implicit stereotypes and attitudes', paper presented at the annual meeting of the Society for Personality and Social Psychology, San Antonio, TX. Cited in Blair, V. (2002) 'The malleability of automatic stereotypes and prejudice', *Personality and Social Psychology Review*, 6(3): 242–61.

Carter, R.T. (1995) *The Influence of Race and Racial Identity in the Psychotherapy Process: Toward a Racially Inclusive Model*. New York: Wiley.

Cass, V. (1979) 'Homosexual identity formation: A theoretical model', *Journal of Homosexuality*, 4(3): 219–35.

Cass, V.C. (1984) 'Homosexuality identity formation: Testing a theoretical model', *Journal of Sex Research*, 20(2): 146–67.

Cezair-Thompson, M. (1999) *The True History of Paradise*. New York: Dutton.

Chang, D. and Berk, A. (2009) 'Making cross-racial therapy work: A phenomenological study of clients' experiences of cross-racial therapy', *Journal of Counseling Psychology*, 56(4): 521–36.

Chaturvedi, S. (2018) *Working with Interpreters in the Counselling Professions*, Good Practice in Action 091 Fact Sheet. Lutterworth: BACP.

Chulov, M. (2014) 'Iraqis stranded on a mountain as Isis jihadists threated death', *The Guardian*, 7 August. Available at: www.theguardian.com/world/2014/aug/07/40000-iraqis-stranded-mountain-isis-death-threat (accessed 7 September 2019).

Cole, O. (2018) *Deaths in Police Custody at Highest Rate for a Decade*. Available at: https://rightsinfo.org/police-custody-deaths-highest-decade/ (accessed 17 August 2019).

Comas-Díaz, L. (2000) 'An ethnopolitical approach to working with people of color', *American Psychologist*, 55: 1319–25.

Comas-Díaz, L. and Greene, B. (eds) (1994) *Women of Color: Integrating Ethnic and Gender Identities in Psychotherapy*. New York: Guilford Press.

Comas-Díaz, L. and Jacobsen, F. (2001) 'Ethnocultural allodynia', *The Journal of Psychotherapy Practice and Research*, 10: 246–52.

Cooley, C.H. (1902) *Human Nature and the Social Order*. New York: Scribner.

Coon, C. (1962) *The Origin of Races*. London: Random House.

Corker, M. (1998) *Deaf and Disabled, or Deafness Disabled?* Buckingham: Open University Press.

Crenshaw, K. (1989) 'Demarginalizing the intersection of race and sex: A black feminist critique of antidiscrimination doctrine, feminist theory and antiracist politics', *University of Chicago Legal Forum*, 1, Article 8: 139–67. Available at: http://chicagounbound.uchicago.edu/uclf/vol1989/iss1/8.

Cross, W. (1971) 'The Negro-to-Black conversion experience', *Black World*, 20(9): 13–27.

Cross, W.E., Jr. (1991) *Shades of Black: Diversity in African-American Identity*. Philadelphia, PA: Temple University Press.

Cross, W. (2016) *How Did We Get Here?* Available at: www.youtube.com/watch?v=F88DG_g2_3A (accessed 15 May 2019).

Davey, E. (2019) 'Two years on from the Windrush scandal, it's clear the Tories have learnt nothing', *Independent*, 21 June. Available at: www.independent.co.uk/voices/windrush-scandal-anniversary-hostile-environment-immigration-a8968861.html (accessed 17 August 2019).

Davies, J. (2019) 'Lessons from the anthropological field: Reflecting on where culture and psychotherapy meet', in K. Martin (ed.), *Psychotherapy, Anthropology and the Work of Culture*. Abingdon: Routledge. pp. 41–66.

Davies, M. (ed.) (1983) Association of African Women for Research and Development (AAWORD) 'A Statement on Genital Mutilation', in M. Davies (ed.), *Third World, Second Sex*. London: Zed Press.

De Beauvoir, S. (1949) *The Second Sex*. New York: Knopf. (Published in English in 1953.)

Degges-White, S., Rice, B. and Myers, J.E. (2000) 'Revisiting Cass' theory of sexual identity development: A study of lesbian development', *Journal of Mental Health Counseling*, 22(4): 318–33.

Desmond, A. and Moore, J. (1991) *Darwin*. London: Michael Joseph.

Devine, P.G. (1989) 'Stereotypes and prejudice: Their automatic and controlled components', *Journal of Experimental Social Psychology*, 56(1): 5–18.

Devine, P.G., Forscher, P.S., Austin, A.J. and Cox, W.T.L. (2012) 'Long-term reduction in implicit race bias: A prejudice habit breaking intervention', *Journal of Experimental Social Psychology*, 48(6): 1267–78.

Devor, A.H. (2004) 'Witnessing and mirroring: A fourteen stage model of transsexual identity formation', *Journal of Gay and Lesbian Psychotherapy*, 8: 41–67.

DiAngelo, R. (2011) 'White fragility', *International Journal of Critical Pedagogy*, 3(3): 54–70.

DiAngelo, R. (2012) *What Does it Mean to be White? Developing White Racial Literacy*. Bern: Peter Lang.

DiAngelo, R. (2018) *White Fragility: Why it's so Hard for White People to Talk about Racism*. Boston, MA: Beacon Press.

Doshi, T. (2010) *The Pleasure Seekers*. London: Bloomsbury.
Dovidio, J.F., Hewstone, M., Gilik, P. and Esses, V. (2010) *The Sage Handbook of Prejudice, Stereotyping and Discrimination*. London: Sage.
Dowling, N.E. and Roush, K.L. (1985) 'From passive acceptance to active commitment: A model of feminist identity development for women', *The Counseling Psychologist*, 13(4): 695–707.
Dreyfus, H.L. and Dreyfus, S. (1986) *Mind Over Machine: The Power of Human Intuition and Expertise in the Era of the Computer*. New York: Free Press.
Du Bois, W.E.B. (1903) *The Souls of Black Folk*. Chicago, IL: A.C. McClurg & Co.
Fairchild, H. (2012) Dr William Cross: 2001 Distinguished Psychologist Address, Denver, CO, 8 March 2001. Available at: www.youtube.com/watch?v=rrozyvu26Ko (accessed 6 September 2019).
Fanon, F. (1952, published in English 1986) *Black Skin, White Masks*. London: Pluto Press.
Farooki, R. (2014) *The Good Children*. London: Tinder Press.
Faye, G. (2016) *Small Country*. London: Hogarth.
Fernando, S. (1991) *Mental Health, Race and Culture*, 1st edn. Basingstoke: Macmillan in association with MIND.
Fernando, S. (2010) *Mental Health, Race and Culture*, 3rd edn. Basingstoke: Palgrave Macmillan.
Forna, A. (2002) *The Devil that Danced on the Water*. New York: HarperCollins.
Forscher, P.S., Mitamura, C., Dix, E.L., Cox, W.T.L. and Devine, P.G. (2017) 'Breaking the prejudice habit: Mechanisms, timecourse, and longevity', *Journal of Experimental Social Psychology*, 72: 133–46.
Freeman, R. (2013) *On Sal Mal Lane*. Minneapolis, MN: Graywolf Press.
Galinsky, A.D. and Moskowitz, G.B. (2000) 'Perspective-taking: Decreasing stereotype expression, stereotype accessibility, and in-group favoritism', *Journal of Personality & Social Psychology*, 78(4): 708–24.
Galton, F. (1883) *Inquiries into Human Faculty*. London: Macmillan.
Gates, H. (1990) 'Critical remark', in D. Goldberg (ed.), *Anatomy of Racism*. Minneapolis, MN: University of Minnesota Press. pp. 319–29.
Georgiadou, L. (2015) '"I was seeing more of her": International counselling trainees' perceived benefits of intercultural clinical practice', *British Journal of Guidance & Counselling*, 43(5): 584–97.
Gibson, J. (2006) 'Disability and clinical competency: An introduction', *The California Psychologist*, 3(9): 6–10.
Global Slavery Index (2019) *2019 MAF Findings: Foreword*. Available at: www.globalslaveryindex.org/2019/findings/foreword/ (accessed 7 September 2019).
Gormley, B. (2018) 'Liberation of bisexual consciousness: Manoeuvring through hostile life environments', *Journal of Bisexuality*, 18(2): 230–48.
Greene, J.C. (1963) *Darwin and the Modern World View*. New York: New American Library.
Haddon, M. (2003) *The Curious Incident of the Dog in the Night-time*. London: Jonathan Cape.
Hannaford, I. (1996) *Race: The History of an Idea in the West*. Washington, DC: Johns Hopkins University Press.
Hardiman, R. and Jackson, B.W. (1997) 'Conceptual foundations for social justice courses', in M. Adams, L.A. Bell and P. Griffin (eds), *Teaching for Diversity and Social Justice: A Sourcebook*. New York: Routledge. pp. 35–66.
Harrison, G., Owens, D., Holton, A., Neilson, D. and Boot, D. (1988) 'A prospective study of severe mental disorder in Afro-Caribbean patients', *Psychological Medicine*, 18: 643–57.

Helms, J.E. (1984) 'Toward a theoretical explanation of the effects of race on counseling: A Black and White model', *The Counseling Psychologist*, 12(4): 153–65.

Helms, J.E. (1995) 'An update of Helms's White and People of Color racial identity models', in J.G. Ponterotto, J.M. Casas, L.A. Suzuki and C.M. Alexander (eds), *Handbook of Multicultural Counseling*. Thousand Oaks, CA: Sage. pp. 181–98.

Herrnstein, R.J. and Murray, C. (1994) *The Bell Curve: Intelligence and Class Structure in American Life*. New York: Free Press.

Home Office (2016) *Home Office's Mandatory Reporting of Female Genital Mutilation: Procedural Information*. Available at: https://assets.publishing.service.gov.uk/government/uploads/system/uploads/attachment_data/file/573782/FGM_Mandatory_Reporting_-_procedural_information_nov16_FINAL.pdf (accessed 11 September 2019).

Howitt, D. and Owusu-Bempah, J. (1994) *The Racism of Psychology*. Hemel Hempstead: Harvester Wheatsheaf.

Huang, H.Y. (2015) 'Therapy and the media in China', *Therapy Today*, 26(7): 8–11.

Iweala, U. (2005) *Beasts of No Nation*. New York: Harper Perennial.

Jackson, J.P. and Weidman, N.M. (2005) *Race, Racism, and Science: Social Impact and Interaction*. New Brunswick, NJ: Rutgers University Press.

Jackson, L. (2002) *Freaks, Geeks, and Asperger Syndrome: A User Guide to Adolescence*. London: Jessica Kingsley.

James, M. (2014) *A Brief History of Seven Killings*. New York: Riverhead Books.

Jardina, A. (2019) *White Identity Politics*. Cambridge: Cambridge University Press.

Joseph, D.P. (1995) '"Nigger bitch"/"dreadlock sister": The experiences of an African-Caribbean woman working in the British National Health Service', *Feminism & Psychology*, 5: 285–9.

Kadare, I. (1978) *Broken April*. New York: Vintage.

Kakoozan, P. in conversation with Boyles, J. (2017) 'Treat us like people', in J. Boyles, *Psychological Therapies for Survivors of Torture*. Monmouth: PCCS. pp. 97–108.

Kearney, A. (2018) *Counselling, Class and Politics: Undeclared Influences in Therapy*, 2nd edn edited by G. Proctor. Monmouth: PCCS.

Khedairi, B. (2007) *Absent*. London: Penguin.

Kidd, D.C. and Castano, E. (2013) 'Reading literary fiction improves theory of mind', *Science*, 342, 18 October. Available at: www.sciencemag.org (accessed 23 February 2019).

Klein, F., Sepekoff, B. and Wolf, T.J. (1985) 'Sexual orientation', *Journal of Homosexuality*, 11(1–2): 35–49.

Kleinman, A. (1995) *Writing at the Margin: Discourse between Anthropology and Medicine*. Berkeley, CA: University of California Press.

Kokaliari, E., Catanzarite, G. and Berzoff, J. (2013) 'It is called a mother tongue for a reason: A qualitative study of therapists' perspectives on bilingual psychotherapy – treatment implications', *Smith College Studies in Social Work*, 83(1): 97–118.

Kucharska, J. (2018) 'Feminist identity styles, sexual and non-sexual traumatic events, and psychological well-being in a sample of Polish women', *Journal of Interpersonal Violence*, 33(1): 117–36.

Ladany, N. and Krikorian, M. (2013) 'Psychotherapy process and social class', in W.M. Liu (ed.), *The Oxford Handbook of Social Class in Counseling*. New York: Oxford University Press. pp. 118–30.

Lahiri, J. (2003) *The Namesake*. Boston, MA: Houghton Mifflin.

Lahiri, J. (2015) *In Other Words*. London: Bloomsbury.

Lawrence, F. (2016) 'Gangmasters agree to pay more than £1m to settle modern slavery claim', *The Guardian*, 20 December. Available at: www.theguardian.com/uk-news/2016/dec/20/gangmasters-agree-1m-payout-to-settle-modern-slavery-claim (accessed 7 September 2019).

Lawson, S.L. and Ramey, S.W. (2018) 'Sourcing stereotypes: Constructing and challenging simplified knowledge', *Culture and Religion*, 19(4): 416–34.
Levy, A. (2004) *Small Island*. London: Headline Review.
Liu, W.M. (2011a) *Social Class and Classism in the Helping Professions: Research, Theory, and Practice*. Thousand Oaks, CA: Sage.
Liu, W.M. (2011b) 'Developing a social class and classism consciousness', in E.M. Altmaier and J.C. Hansen (eds), *The Oxford Handbook of Counseling Psychology*. New York: Oxford University Press. pp. 326–45.
Liu, W.M. (ed.) (2013) *The Oxford Handbook of Social Class in Counseling*. New York: Oxford University Press.
Mackie, D.M., Devos, T. and Smith, E.R. (2000) 'Intergroup emotions: Explaining offensive action tendencies in an intergroup context', *Journal of Personality and Social Psychology*, 79: 602–16.
Macpherson, W. (1999) *The Stephen Lawrence Inquiry*. London: Home Office. Available at: https://assets.publishing.service.gov.uk/government/uploads/system/uploads/attachment_data/file/277111/4262.pdf (accessed 23 March 2019).
Malek, A. (2017) *The Home that was Our Country: A Memoir of Syria*. Emeryville, CA: Avalon.
Markle, M. (2015) 'I'm more than an "Other"', *Elle*, July. Available at: www.elle.com/uk/life-and-culture/news/a26855/more-than-an-other/ (accessed 15 May 2019).
Matar, H. (2006) *In the Country of Men*. London: Viking.
Matar, H. (2016) *The Return: Fathers, Sons and the Land in Between*. London: Penguin.
Matthews-King, A. (2019) 'Universal Credit "ruining lives" and making mental health patients more ill report warns', *Huffington Post*, 4 March. Available at: www.huffingtonpost.co.uk/entry/universal-credit-terminal-illness-number-claims-revealed_u (accessed 17 August 2019).
McCarn, S.R. and Fassinger, R.E. (1996) 'Revisioning sexual minority identity formation: A new model of lesbian identity and its implications for counseling and research', *The Counseling Psychologist*, 24(3): 508–34.
McIntosh, P. (1988) 'White privilege and male privilege: A personal account of coming to see correspondences through work in women's studies', Wellesley: Center for Research on Women. Working paper 189. Republished as McIntosh, P. (2003) 'White privilege: Unpacking the invisible knapsack', in S. Plous (ed.), *Understanding Prejudice and Discrimination*. New York: McGraw-Hill. pp. 191–6.
McKenzie-Mavinga, I. (2016) *The Challenge of Racism in Therapeutic Practice: Engaging with Oppression in Practice and Supervision*. London: Palgrave Macmillan.
McVeigh, T. (2016) 'Why activists brought the Black Lives Matter movement to the UK', *The Guardian*, 6 August. Available at: www.theguardian.com/uk-news/2018/dec/18/sheku-bayoh-calls-for-inquiry-after-new-cctv-of-arrest-emerges (accessed 17 August 2019).
Mead, M. with an introduction by M. Pipher (2004) *Coming of Age in Samoa: A Psychological Study of Primitive Youth for Western Civilization*. New York: Perennial Classics. (1st edn 1928.)
Mengiste, M. (2010) *Beneath the Lion's Gaze*. New York: Norton.
Metzi, J. (2010) *The Protest Psychosis: How Schizophrenia became a Black Disease*. Boston, MA: Beacon Press.
Mistry, R. (2003) *Family Matters*. London: Penguin.
Moodley, R. and West, W. (2005) *Integrating Traditional Healing Practices into Counselling and Psychotherapy*. Thousand Oaks, CA: Sage.
Murray, C. (1996) *Charles Murray and the Underclass: The Developing Debate*. Available at: www.civitas.org.uk/pdf/cw33.pdf (accessed 7 September 2019).

Newman, L.S. and Caldwell, T.L. (2005) 'Allport's "Living Inkblots": The role of defensive projection in stereotyping and prejudice', in J.F. Dovidio, P. Glick and L.A. Rudman (eds), *The Dynamics of Prejudice: Fifty Years after Allport*. Oxford: Blackwell. pp. 377–92.

Parliament, House of Commons (2014) *The Government Response to the House of Commons Home Affairs Committee Report: Female Genital Mutilation: Follow-up*. London: The Stationery Office Limited.

Parliament, House of Commons (2015) *Home Affairs Committee Follow-up Report on Female Genital Mutilation*. London: The Stationery Office Limited.

Pearson (2015) *Nursing: A Concept-Based Approach to Learning*, Vol. 1, 2nd edn. Boston: Pearson.

Phinney, J. (1990) 'Ethnic identity in adolescents and adults: Review of research', *Psychological Bulletin*, 108: 499–514.

Popoola, O. (2017) *When we Speak of Nothing*. London: Cassava Press.

Poston, W.S.C. (1990) 'The biracial identity development model: A needed addition', *Journal of Counseling and Development*, 69(2): 152–5.

Poussaint, A.F. (2002) 'Is extreme racism a mental illness? Yes: It can be a delusional symptom of psychotic disorders', *Western Journal of Medicine*, 176(1): 1467–85.

Premack, D. and Woodruff, G. (1978) 'Chimpanzee theory of mind: Part I. Perception of causality and purpose in the child and chimpanzee', *Behavioral and Brain Science*, 1(4): 616–29.

Proctor, G. (2006) 'Therapy: Opium of the masses or help for those who need it least?', in G. Proctor, P. Sanders, M. Cooper and B. Malcolm (eds), *Politicizing the Person-centred Approach: An Agenda for Social Change*. Ross-on-Wye: PCCS Books. pp. 66–79.

Renn, K.A. (2008) 'Research on biracial and multiracial identity development: Overview and synthesis', *New Directions for Student Service*, 23: 13–21.

Rich, K.R. (2011) *Dreaming in Hindi: Life in Translation*. London: Portobello Books.

Root, M.P.P. (1990) 'Resolving "Other" status: Identity development of biracial individuals', *Women & Therapy*, 9: 185–205.

Ross, L. (2011) *The Origin of the Term 'Women of Color'*. Available at: www.youtube.com/watch?v=82vl34mi4lw (accessed 28 August 2019).

Ryan, F. (2019) *Crippled: Austerity and the Demonization of Disabled People*. London: Verso.

Ryan, J. (2006) '"Class is in you": An exploration of some social class issues in psychotherapeutic work', *British Journal of Psychotherapy*, 23(1): 49–62.

Ryan, J. (2017) *Class and Psychoanalysis: Landscapes of Inequality*. London: Karnac.

Said, E. (1978) *Orientalism*. New York: Pantheon Books.

Sanghera, S. (2013) *Marriage Material*. London: Windmill.

Sauer, N. (1992) 'Forensic anthropology and the concept of race: If races don't exist, why are forensic anthropologists so good at identifying them?', *Social Science and Medicine*, 34(2): 107–11.

Savage, M., Warde, A. and Devine, F. (2005) 'Capitals, assets, and resources: Some critical issues', *The British Journal of Sociology*, 56(1): 31–47.

Savage, M., Devine, F., Cunningham, N., Taylor, M., Li, Y., Hjellbrekke, J., Le Roux, B., Friedman, S. and Miles, A. (2013) 'A new model of social class: Findings from the BBC's Great British Class Survey experiment', *Sociology*, 47(2): 219–50.

Schalk, S. (2016) 'Reevaluating the supercrip', *Journal of Literary and Cultural Disability Studies*, 10(1): 71–86.

Schick, V.R., Brandi, N., Rima, B.N. and Calabrese, S.K. (2011) 'Evulvalution: The portrayal of women's external genitalia and physique across time and the current Barbie doll ideals', *Journal of Sex Research*, 48(1): 74–81.

Shah, K. (2019) 'They look white but say they're black: A tiny town in Ohio struggles with race', *The Guardian*, 25 July. Available at: https://www.theguardian.com/us-news/2019/jul/25/race-east-jackson-ohio-appalachia-white-black?CMP=share_btn_fb&fbclid=IwAR-1BIQTOpP_20JW4I-ttIKEZLZiLb-5UTp2IQyKfDdpJar7v93uIxthhz9I (accessed 6 September 2019).

Shakespeare, T. (2002) 'The social model of disability: An outdated ideology?', *Research in Social Science and Disability*, 2: 9–28.

Shoneye, T. (2018) 'As a black woman, I hate the term "People of Colour"', *Independent*, 22 April. Available at: www.independent.co.uk/voices/black-women-people-of-colour-racism-beyonce-coachella-black-lives-matter-a8316561.html (accessed 28 August 2019).

Simoni, J.M. and Walters, K.L. (2001) 'Heterosexual identity and heterosexism: Recognizing privilege to reduce prejudice', *Journal of Homosexuality*, 41(1): 157–72.

Skeggs, B. (1997) *Formations of Class and Gender: Becoming Respectable*. London: Sage.

Smith, L.C. (2015) 'Alterity models in counseling: When we talk about diversity, what are we actually talking about?', *International Journal of Advanced Counselling*, 37: 248–61.

Solomon, A. (2008) 'Depression, too, is a thing with feathers', *Contemporary Psychoanalysis*, 44(4): 509–30.

Splevins, K.A., Cohen, K., Joseph, J., Murray, C. and Bowley, J. (2010) 'Vicarious posttraumatic growth among interpreters', *Qualitative Health Research*, 20(12): 1705–16.

Steele, C. (2010) *Whistling Vivaldi: And Other Clues as to How Stereotypes Affect Us*. New York: Norton.

Stephan, N. (1982) *The Idea of Race in Science*. London: Macmillan.

Stephan, W.G. and Stephan, C.W. (1985) 'Intergroup anxiety', *Journal of Social Issues*, 41(3): 157–75.

Stonequist, E.V. (1961) *The Marginal Man: A Study in Personality and Culture Conflict*. New York: Russell and Russell.

Sue, D.W. and Sue, D. (2016) *Counseling the Culturally Diverse*, 7th edn. Hoboken, NJ: Wiley.

Summers, H. and Ratcliffe, R. (2019) 'Mother of three-year-old is first person convicted of FGM in UK', *The Guardian*, 1 February. Available at: www.theguardian.com/society/2019/feb/01/fgm-mother-of-three-year-old-first-person-convicted-in-uk (accessed 10 September 2019).

Tajfel, H. (1969) 'Cognitive aspects of prejudice', *Journal of Biosocial Science*, 1(1): 173–91.

Tajfel, H. and Turner, J.C. (1979) 'An integrative theory of intergroup conflict', in W.G. Austin and S. Worchel (eds), *The Social Psychology of Intergroup Relations*. Monterey, CA: Brooks/Cole.

Tannen, D. (1991) *You Just Don't Understand: Women and Men in Conversation*. New York: Ballantine.

Terbeck, S., Kahane, G., McTavish, S., Savulescu, J., Cowen, P.J. and Hewstone, M. (2012) 'Propranolol reduces implicit negative racial bias', *Psychopharmacology*, 222(3): 419–24.

Tervalon, M. and Murray-García, J. (1998) 'Cultural humility versus cultural competence: A critical distinction in defining physician training outcomes in multicultural education', *Journal of Health Care for the Poor and Underserved*, 9(2): 117–25.

The Children's Society (2017) *Claiming after Care: Care Leavers and the Benefits System*. Available at: www.childrenssociety.org.uk/sites/default/files/claiming-after-care-care-leavers-and-the-benefits-system_0.pdf (accessed 17 August 2019).

Thomas, C.W. (1971) *Boys No More*. Beverly Hills, CA: Glencoe Press.
Tolan, J. with Cameron, R. (2017) *Skills for Person Centred Counselling and Psychotherapy*, 3rd edn. London: Sage.
Townsend, M. (2016) 'Homophobic attacks in UK rose 147% in three months after Brexit vote', *The Guardian*, 8 October. Available at: www.theguardian.com/society/2016/oct/08/homophobic-attacks-double-after-brexit-vote (accessed 20 May 2019).
Travis, A. (2016) 'Lasting rise in hate crime after EU referendum, figures show', *The Guardian*, 7 September. Available at: www.theguardian.com/society/2016/sep/07/hate-surgedafter-eu-referendum-police-figures-show (accessed 20 May 2019).
Trawalter, S., Adam, E.K., Chase-Lansdale, P.L. and Richeson, J.A. (2012) 'Concerns about appearing prejudiced get under the skin: Stress responses to interracial contact in the moment and across time', *Journal of Experimental Social Psychology*, 48: 682–93.
Troiden, R. (1989) 'The formation of homosexual identities', *Journal of Homosexuality*, 17(1–2): 43–74.
Trott, A. (2016) *Social Class and the Therapeutic Relationship: The Client's Perspective*. Unpublished MSc thesis. University of Chester, United Kingdom.
Tudor, K. and Naughton, M. (2006) 'Being white', *Transactional Analysis Journal*, 36(2): 159–71.
Tyler, I. and Bennett, B. (2010) '"Celebrity chav": Fame, femininity and social class', *European Journal of Cultural Studies*, 13(3): 375–93.
Tylor, E.B. (1920 [1871]) *Primitive Culture: Researches into the Development of Mythology, Philosophy, Religion, Language, Art, and Custom*, Vol. 1. London: John Murray.
United Nations (2015) *Office of the High Commissioner for Human Rights: Free & Equal Campaign Fact Sheet: Intersex*. Available at: www.unfe.org/wp-content/uploads/2017/05/UNFE-Intersex.pdf (accessed 12 September 2019).
Vandiver, B.J. (2001) 'Psychological nigrescence revisited: Introduction and overview', *Journal of Multicultural Counseling and Development*, 29: 165–73.
Wainaina, B. (2006) 'How to write about Africa', *Granta 92*. Available at: https://granta.com/how-to-write-about-africa/ (accessed 27 August 2019).
Wainaina, B. (2011) *One Day I Will Write About This Place*. London: Granta.
Ward, V. (2018) 'UK's welfare system is cruel and misogynistic, says UN expert after damning report on poverty', *Telegraph*, 16 November. Available at: www.telegraph.co.uk/news/2018/11/16/welfare-system-cruel-misogynistic-un-expert-warns-damning-report/ (accessed 27 August 2019).
Williams, C. (2014) *Gender Performance: The Transadvocate Interviews Judith Butler*, 1 May. Available at: http://transadvocate.com/gender-performance-the-transadvocate-interviews-judith-butler_n_13652.htm (accessed 12 September 2019).
Williams, M. (2014) 'Can a White person understand the Black experience?', *Psychology Today*. Available at: www.psychologytoday.com/gb/blog/culturally-speaking/201408/can-white-person-understand-the-black-experience (accessed 31 August 2019).
Youle, E. (2019) 'Universal Credit: Number of terminally ill people forced to claim benefit revealed', *Huffpost*, 17 June. Available at: https://www.huffingtonpost.co.uk/entry/universal-credit-terminal-illness-number-claims-revealed_uk_5d078b59e4b0dc17ef-0d2886?guccounter=1&guce_referrer=aHR0cHM6Ly93d3cuZ29vZ2xlLmNvbS8&-guce_referrer_sig=AQAAAGThOTnOpr47Fs6qofgr-_c2qTRYQzibF3T69e8wiivhuGCZGwl-WDMpreXgPB7IA6IAcBRb4RBxFbWjzmxcctCutZtBPcOi1LptvM52I6X4yCTtQs9NcCflAPN 6w3oW-Jf97YXQqkby_q_Wy3yt-jpViWBiripUQ7_Ek5H2wlF9e (accessed 17 August 2019).

Index

Abdolah, Kader 99
Absent (Khedairi) 99
Abu-Lughod, Lila 104
Academic Disability Studies 36
acceptance 54, 59
Achebe, Chinwa 98
active commitment 50
adaption 56
additional languages 138–9
Addonia, Sulaiman 99
Adébáyo, Ayòbámi 98
Adichie, Chimamanda Ngozi 98, 99
advice giving 89–90
aesthetic attraction 67
age 37–8
agender 68
Akala 65
aliagender 68
allodynia 9
Allport, Gordon 113, 116, 117
ally 70
American Civil Rights era 14
American Psychiatric Association (APA) 14–15, 35
Anam, Tahmima 98
androgyne 68
angst and ambivalence 59
anti-miscegenation laws 64
Aries, Elizabeth and Maynard Seider 75
ars erotica 35–6
asexuality 66–7
Asian identity 20
Aslam, Nadeem 98
Association of African Women for Research and Development 106
Atta, Sefi 98
austerity 41
authoritative generalisations 92
Autonomy, white identity status 127
aversive racism 118

Balmforth, Jane 145
Bassey, Suki and Steve Melluish 90–1
Beasts of No Nation (Iweala) 99
bedroom tax 75–6
Bell Curve: Intelligence and Class Structure in American Life, The (Murray) 24
Beneath the Lion's Gaze (Mengiste) 99
Bernstein, Basil 135
bias 112–14, 114–15, 118
  see also implicit bias
bigender 68
Binkley, Jessica 100
biological race theory 26

biracial identity 64
Biracial Identity Development Model 64–5
bisexual identity development models 66
Bisexual Movement 66
bisexuality 66
black identity development theories 46–9
black men, paranoid schizophrenia and 14
Black Power 52
black women 77–8
blackness tests 59
Bliss, Catherine 26
Blumenbach, J.F. 20, 24
Bockting et al. 146
bol 68
Boochani, Behrouz 98
Bourdieu, Pierre 39
Boyles, Jude and Nathalie Talbot 140, 141, 143, 144
Brexit 6
Brief History of Seven Killings, A (James) 98
British Association for Counselling and Psychotherapy (BACP) 106
Broken April (Kadare) 97
Burn, Louise 99
butch 68
Butler, Judith 33, 68

Carmichael, Stokely 122
Carpenter, S. and Banaji, M.R. 115
Carter, Robert 12, 47, 59
Cass, Vivienne 52
celebrity culture 39
celibacy 66
Cezair-Thompson, Margaret 98
Chang, Doris and Alexandra Berk 145, 146
charmed circle 123–5
Chartered Institute of Linguists (CIOL) 140
child abuse 105
chronic stress 12
circumcision, female 104–5, 106
cisgender 70
Civil Rights Movement 52
class 38–40
  changing identities 74–5
  therapeutic relationships 145
class identity development models 55–8
Clinton, President Bill 25
cognitive revolution 114–15
collectivism 88
colonisation 13
colour-blindness 123
Comas-Díaz, Lillian and Beverley Greene 13
Comas-Díaz, Lillian and Frederick Jacobsen 9
coming out 51, 52

communication 133–44
  case study 136
  frames and filters 136–7
  speaking in code 135
  working in an additional language 138–9
  working with an interpreter 139–44
    before therapy begins 141–2
    contracting with the client 142
    post-session 143–4
    session 142–3
  see also language
complementary projection 117
Complex Post-Colonisation Stress Disorder 13
confession 36
Contact, white identity status 126
contemporary identities 63–81
  asexuality 66–7
  case studies 65–6, 70–1, 72, 73–4, 75–7, 78–9
  changing class identities 74–5
  disability 72–4
  dos and don'ts 80–1
  drawing your own box 64–5
  from Gay Lib to LGBTQQIAAP+ 66
  gender non-conforming 67–71
  intersectionality 77–8
  intersex 71
  pansexuality, polysexuality, skoliosexuality and questioning 67
contracts 142
conversion therapies 34–5
Cooley, Charles Horton 46
Coon, Carlton 22
Corker, Mairian 73
counselling 88
counter-stereotypic imaging 115
In the Country of Men (Matar) 99
Crenshaw, Kimberlé 77–8
Cross, Professor William 21, 46, 49
cross-racial relationships 128
crossed relationship 128
Cukor, George Dewey 10
cultural arrogance 85–92
  advice giving 89–90
  case studies 89, 90, 91
  knowledge 90–1
  therapeutic approaches 86–8
cultural capital 39
cultural competence 101
cultural errors 100
cultural humility 93–102
  listening to the 'other' 96–101
cultural imperialism 86
cultural knowledge 96
culture 94–5
  ambivalence towards 94
  case studies 94, 95, 97, 101
  demonising and romanticising 103–8
  doing of 96
  female genital mutilation (FGM) 104–5
  literary fiction and 96–100
  nature of 95
  subcultures 94
Curious Incident of the Dog in the Night-time, The (Haddon) 73

Cuvier, Georges 21–2
Cyrus, Miley 67

Darwin, Charles 22, 24–5
Darwinism 24
Davies, James 96
de Beauvoir, Simone 32
deaf community 37
deconstruction 123
Degges-White et al. 52
demiboy 68
demigirl 68
demisexuals 67
demonising the other 103–8
denial and acceptance 59
Desai, Anita 98
Descent of Man, The (Darwin) 25
Desmond, A. and Moore, J. 24
Devil that Danced on the Water, The (Forna) 99
Devine et al. 115, 116
Devine, Patricia 114, 115
Devor, Aaron 70
DiAngelo, Robin 113–14, 125
difference-blindness 123
direct projection 117
disability 36–7
  identity and 72–4
  medical model 36, 53, 73
  nothing about us without us model 53–5
  social model 36–7, 53–4, 73
disability identity development models 54–5
Disability Rights Movement 36, 54
disabled people 54
  exclusion 37
  poverty and 41
  see also people with disabilities
discourse 122, 123
discrimination 6
disease 26
Disintegration, white identity status 126
displaced aggression 117
distress 86
DNA 26
Doshi, Tishani 97
double consciousness 46
Dovidio et al. 118
Dowling, Nancy and Kristin Roush 49–50
drawing your own box 64–5
Dreaming in Hindi: Life in Translation (Russell Rich) 139
Dreyfus, Hubert and Stuart 100
DSM (Diagnostic and Statistical Manual of Mental Disorders) 5 12
Du Bois, W.E.B. 46
dual heritage 65
dyslexia 74

Eastern cultures 90–1
economic capital 39
economic inequality 6
Edmonstone, John 24–5
Ego Dystonic Homosexuality 35
ego statuses 46–7
elaborated code 135
elite class 39

embeddedness-emanation 50
emergent service workers 40
emotion 116
enby 68
Encounter-Dissonance 47
enculturation 85–92
enslaved labour 23
erotic arts 35–6
established middle class 39
ethnic groups 28, 103
ethnicity 27–8
ethnocultural allodynia 9
Eugenics Movement 24
Evaristo, Bernardine 98
evolution, theory of 25
exclusion, of disabled people 37
exploration 56
external/distal stressors 11

false consciousness 46
Family Matters (Mistry) 97
Fanon, Frantz 111
Farooki, Roopa 98
Faye, Gael 99
female circumcision 104–5, 106
female genital mutilation (FGM) 104–6
    and child abuse 105
    reporting of 107
female to male (FTM) 68
feminine-of-centre 68
feminine presenting 68
feminism 32, 49–50, 52
feminist identity development model 49–50
Fernando, Suman 122
fiction 96–100
filters 136–7
food banks 40, 76
Forna, Aminatta 99
Foucault, Michel 35–6, 122, 123
frames 136–7
Freaks, Geeks and Asperger Syndrome (Jackson) 73
Freeman, Ru 98, 99
Freud, Sigmund 95, 117

gaslighting 10
gay gene 34
gay identity development models 51–3
Gay Liberation Movement 51, 52, 66
gender 32–4
    performative 33
    roles 32
gender creative 68
gender expression 70
gender fluid 68
gender identity 70
gender neutral 68
gender non-conforming 67–71
gender questioning 68
gender variant 68
genderless 68
Gendlin, Eugene 95
General Data Protection Regulation (GDPR) 142
genital cosmetic surgery (GCS) 104–5, 106
genomes 25

genomic research 25–6
Georgiadou, Lorena 138
Gibson, Jennifer 54
gig economy 41
Gilligan, Carol 32
glad to be gay 51–3
Good Children, The (Farooki) 98
Gormley, Barbara 66
Great British Class Survey (2011) 39
Great British Class Survey (2015) 75
Great Chain of Being 21
grey asexuals 66–7

Half of a Yellow Sun (Adichie) 99
Hardiman, R. and Jackson, B.W. 125, 128, 129
Harlan, John Marshal 123
hatred 11–12, 14–16
Helms, Janet 46–7, 49, 125, 128
Herrnstein, Richard 24
heteronormativity 66
heterosexuality 66
hidden disabilities 73
hierarchical framing 136
Holocaust 24
Home that was our Country: A Memoir of Syria, The (Malek) 98
homelessness 40
homosexuality 35, 66
honour killings 97
Hosseini, Khaled 98
hostility 5–18
    allegory 6
    case study 8–9
    hatred 11–12, 14–16
    intergenerational transmission of trauma 13
    microaggressions 7–11
        deniability of 11
    microassaults 8
    microinsults 8–9, 11
    microinvalidations 9–11
    minority stress 11–12, 13–14
    other 7
House of the Mosque, The (Abdolah) 99
human rights, denial of 28
Hussein, Leyla 105

identity 45–61
    becoming a woman 49–51
    becoming black 46–9
    becoming glad to be gay 51–3
    case studies 48, 50–1, 52, 54–5, 56–8
    class 55–8
    nothing about us without us model 53–5
    practising with care 58–60
    psychodynamic perspective of 46
    psychosocial perspective of 46
    see also contemporary identities
identity acceptance 52
identity comparison 52
identity confusion 52
identity pride 52
identity purgatory 64
identity synthesis 52
identity tolerance 52

ideology 122, 123
Immersion-Emersion status 47, 127
impairment 36–7, 72–3
implicit bias 114–15, 116, 118
incongruence 56
indentured labour 22–3
indigenous peoples 21
individualism 88
individuating 115, 116
institutional discrimination 122
institutional racism 122
Integrating Traditional Healing Practices into Counselling and Psychotherapy (Moodley and West) 108
integration 56
intelligence 24
intergender 68
intergenerational transmission of trauma 13
intergroup anxiety 118
Intergroup Emotions Theory 117
internal/proximal stressors 11–12
Internalisation-Commitment 47–8
internalised oppression 46
International Classification of Diseases (ICD-11) 12
interpreters 139–44
interracial relationships 64
intersectionality 77–8
intersex people 33, 71
Iweala, Uzodinma 99

James, Marlon 98
Jardina, Ashley 131
Jim Crow laws 21
Joseph, Dionne 59

Kakoozan, Prossy 86–7, 98, 100
Kearney, Anne 55, 75, 135
Kerr, Will 23
Khedairi, Betool 99
kick the cat syndrome 117
Kidd, David and Emanuele Castano 96
Klein et al. 66
Kleinman, Arthur 95
knowledge 90–1
Kokaliari et al. 138, 139
Koslofsky, Shahana 100

labiaplasty 104–5
Ladany, Nicholas and Maryann Krikorian 55–6
Lahiri, Jhumpa 97, 98, 139
Lamming, George 98
language 123, 133–4
  additional 138–9
  see also communication
laser vaginal rejuvenation 104–5
Lawrence, Stephen 122
Lawson, Sierra and Steven Ramey 92
lesbians 52
Levy, Andrea 98
LGBTQQIAAP+ 66
literary fiction 96–100
Liu, William 55, 56
looking-glass self 46

Mackintosh, Peggy 124
Macpherson, Sir William 122
majority racial identity models 125–9
male to female (MTF) 68
Malek, Alia 98
Mandatory Reporting of Female Genital Mutilation – Procedural Information (2016) 107
mansplaining 8
marginalised identity development models 46–9, 58–60
Marriage Material (Sanghera) 97
Marx, Karl 55
masculine-of-centre 68
masculine presenting 68
masturbation 67
Matar, Hisham 99
May, Theresa 6
McCarn, Susan and Ruth Fassinger 52
Mead, Margaret 32, 33
medical model of disability 36, 53, 73
Meghan, Duchess of Sussex 64
Mengiste, Maaza 99
mental disorders 14–15
Metzi, Jonathan 14
microaggressions 7–11
microassaults 8
microinsults 8–9, 11
microinvalidations 9–11
middle classes 39, 74–5
Milkman, The (Burn) 99
minority stress 11–12, 13–14
misgendering 123
Mistry, Rohinton 97
mixed race 65, 66
mononormativity 66
Murray, Charles 24
Mx 68

Namesake, The (Lahiri) 97
National Register of Communication Professionals working with Deaf and Deafblind People 140
National Register of Public Service Interpreters 140
nationality 28
nationality status 28
natural selection 25
naturalists 20, 21–2
  research and 24
Nature of Prejudice, The (Allport) 113
NB 68
Negro-to-Black conversion 46
negroes 24
neutrols 68
new affluent workers 40, 75
Newman, L.S. and Caldwell, T.L. 116
No Friend but the Mountains: Writing from Manus Prison (Boochani) 98
non-binary 68
nothing about us without us model 53–5
Nuremberg Laws (1935) 24
Nwaubani, Adaobi Tricia 98

Okri, Ben 98
omnisexuality 67
One Day I Will Write About This Place (Wainaina) 97
one drop rule 21

opportunities for contact 115
Orbach, Susie 66
Orientalism 108
Origin of the Species, The (Darwin) 25
other 7
    demonising and romanticising 103–8
    listening to 96–101
    stereotypes of 112–13
over-sensitivity 9
Oyeyemi, Helen 98

pangender 68
pansexuality 67
parallel relationship 128
paranoid schizophrenia 14
passive acceptance 50
passive awareness 54
people of colour 134
people with disabilities 54
    see also disabled people
perspective taking 115
Phinney, Jean 49
plantations 22
    owners 22, 23
Pleasure Seekers, The (Doshi) 97
political correctness 59
polygender 68
polysexuality 67
Popoola, Olumide 98
post-class 6
post-race 6
Post Traumatic Stress Disorder (PTSD) model 12
Postcolonial Studies 108
Poston, Carlos 64–5
poverty 6–7, 40–1
power 112, 122–3, 123
Pre-awareness-Unexamined identity 47
precariat 40, 75
prejudice 111–18, 121–2
    bias and 112–14
    changing your mind 114–16
    emotion and 116
    Implicit 112–14
pride stage 52
privilege 121–31
Proctor, Gillian 145
progressive relationship 128
Project Implicit 114
projection 117
Pseudo-independence, white identity status 127
psychoanalytic thinking 116
psychodynamic perspective of identity 46
psychological impact of hostility *see* hostility
psychology, race and 23–4
psychosocial perspective of identity 46
psychotherapeutic colonisation 13

queer 70
questioning 67

race
    biology and 22, 24, 25–7
    as a community perception 21
    disease and 26
    intelligence and 24
    invention of 20–2
    psychology and 23–4
    science and 25
    social reality of 27
Race-Based Traumatic Stress Injury model 12
race-free science 26
race-positive science 26
race theory 20, 21
racial categories 20, 21
racial hierarchy 21
racial identity development models 46–9, 64, 65
racism
    medication for 15
    as a mental disorder 14–15, 16
    psychological damage 12
    us and them thinking 16
reactivated trauma 144
realisation 54
reflexivity 41
regressive relationship 128
Reintegration, white identity status 127
religion 29
Renn, Kristen 65
research, uses and abuses of 24–5
respect, lack of 8, 9
restricted code 135
Return: Fathers, Sons and the Land in Between, The (Matar) 99
revelation 50
Rogers, Carl 94
role power 112
romanticising the other 103–8
Root, Maria 65
Roy, Anuradha 98
Roy, Arundhati 98
Royal College of Midwives 106
Russell Rich, Katherine 139
Ryan, Joanna 55, 75, 145

Sahota, Sunjeev 98
Said, Edward 108
On Sal Mal Lane (Freeman) 99
same-sex marriages 66
Sanghera, Sathnam 91, 97
Savage et al. 74–5
Savage, Mike 39
savages 21
schizophrenia 14, 122
    diagnostic criteria 14
science of sexuality 35–6
science, race and 25
scientia sexualis 35–6
scientific race theory 26
secondary trauma 144
self-esteem 49
Selvon, Sam 98
sex 33
sexual orientation 51
Sexual Orientation Disturbance (SOD) 35
sexuality 34–6, 66
Shah, K. 21
Shakespeare, Tom 72–3
Shoneyin, Titilola Alexandrah 98

Shukla, Nikesh 98
sickle cell anaemia 26
sign language 140
sign language interpreters 142–3
Silence is my Mother Tongue (Addonia) 99
Simoni, Jane and Karina Walters 128
simplified knowledge 92, 137, 138
Skeggs, Beverley 8, 10, 38, 75
skoliosexuality 67
slavery 22–3
slaves 21
Small Country (Faye) 99
Small Island (Levy) 98
social capital 39
Social Class and Classism Consciousness Model 56
Social Class Worldview Model 56
social constructionist view 41
　age 37–8
　class 38–40
　disability 36–7
　ethnicity 27–8
　gender 32–4
　nationality 28
　poverty 40–1
　race 20–4, 25–7
　religion 29
　sex 34
　sexuality 34–6
Social Darwinism 25
Social Identity Development Model 125, 128
Social Identity Theory 117
social imagery 112
social inequality 14
social justice approach 12
social learning 32
social mobility 39
social model of disability 36–7, 53–4, 73
social power 112
social stratification 133
Solomon, Andrew 86
Spencer, Herbert 25
Splevins et al. 144
squeezed middle 41
Steele, Claude 11
Stephan, W.G. and Stephan, C.W. 118
stereotype replacement 115, 116
stereotypes 11, 112–13
Stewart, Kristen 67
Stonequist, Everett 64
Sue, Derald Wing and David Sue 89
survival of the fittest 25
symbolic capital 39
syndrome 12
synthesis 50
systemic racism 122

Tajfel, H. and Turner, J.C. 117
Tajfel, Henri 113
Tanega, Preti 98
Tannen, Deborah 136
taxidermy 24
technical middle class 39

Tervalon, Melanie and Jann Murray-Garcia 101
therapeutic methods 86–8
therapeutic relationships 13, 14, 145–7
　being comfortable 59–60
　class and 145
therapists 88
therapy 7, 100
third gender 68
traditional healing 108
traditional working class 40
trans 68
trans clients 134
transfeminine 68
transgender 68–9
transman 70
transmasculine 70
transsexual 70
transwoman 70
trauma 13, 139, 144
Trawalter et al. 118
trigender 70
Troiden, Richard 52
Trott, A. 146
True History of Paradise, The (Cezair-Thompson) 98
Trump, President Donald 6
Tyler, Imogen and Bruce Bennett 39
Tylor, Edward Burnett 103

unconscious bias 114
unconscious prejudice 114
unearned privileges 124
United Nations 33
United Nations Special Rapporteur 6–7
Universal Credit 7, 76
us and them thinking 16, 52

vicarious trauma 144

Wainaina, Binyavanga 97, 138
Western cultures 90–1
When we Speak of Nothing (Popoola) 98
white fragility 125
white privilege 22–3
White Racial Identity Model 125, 126
　Autonomy status 127
　Contact status 126
　Disintegration status 126
　Immersion-Emersion status 127
　Pseudo-independence status 127
　Reintegration status 127
white racial identity models 125–9
　case study 129–30
whiteness 131
Williams, Monnica 146–7
Windrush Scandal 6
women, identity of 49–51
working class(es) 40, 74–5
　poverty and 40
Working with Interpreters in Psychological Therapy (Boyles and Talbot) 140
Working with Interpreters in the Counselling Professions (BACP) 143